Fashion Spaces
A Theoretical View

T0124902

FRAME

Contents

Contents

Foreword: The Ideation of Fashion Spaces

Text
Vésma Kontere McQuillan

From a query ...

Over the last 20 years, the Milan-based fashion house Prada
has created very different collections each season, both for
the catwalk and for the retail market. Traditionally, established
fashion houses have a signature look and signature products –
for instance Chanel's tweed suits – and these don't change
much over the years. Prada, on the other hand, can be defined
by constant surprise, fuelled by its intellectual approach to
aesthetics. It absorbs ideas from other fields, such as contemporary art and cinema, and translates them into clothes. Prada is
not about how products look – it is about the message they carry.

    The first Prada fashion show to be live-streamed was Fall/
Winter 2010, which was staged during Men's Fashion Week in
Milan. This was also the first of its shows in which the womenswear
collection was presented together with the men's collection, and
it was a much larger event than any of Prada's previous shows.
The dominant pattern in both collections was camouflage – it
seemed to imply that the fashion industry was still in hiding from
the fundamental changes needed to flourish in the internet era.
Seven years later, I interviewed Alexander Reichert, who had
been working for the Rotterdam-based architectural office OMA/
AMO at the time – from 2004 until his departure in 2011 he was
the project leader for the office's collaboration with Prada.[1] When
we spoke, he emphasised that the decision to live-stream the
event reflected the brand's determination to reach bigger audiences not just through expanding its collections, but also, and
perhaps more importantly, by leveraging digital channels.

    I soon got into the habit of watching the live-stream of every
Prada show. At some point, I noticed that I was developing a very
personal connection to the products presented. Later, when I

---

1   Alexander Reichert, interview by Vésma Kontere McQuillan, Basel, 7 February 2017.

          Foreword

visited Prada stores, I felt I was already familiar with the styles – they seemed to hold certain memories for me. This made me question what really happens during those brief few minutes at a fashion show. Certainly, storytelling plays an important role in catching the viewer's attention, just as it does in theatre. The leading couturiers of the early 20th century, Paul Poiret and Lucile, both claimed to have created the first fashion shows, and both also said that they had been inspired by contempo-rary theatre in doing so.[2] But I began to feel that fashion shows might be something more than just theatrical performances with a distinctive approach to scenography – there was something more, and I wanted to know what it was.

… to a collaboration …

Every fashion show can be seen as a microcosm that offers perspectives on society, culture, art, architecture and fashion. With this in mind, I decided to try and unravel the collaboration between two of the most remarkable creators of architecture and fashion in our time: OMA/AMO, led by the Dutch architect Rem Koolhaas, and Prada, led by the Italian fashion designer Miuccia Prada. AMO acts as the research arm of OMA, and has been working with Prada since 1999. The partnership began with the design of Prada's retail outlets in New York, Los Angeles and San Francisco, and this has been well described by Koolhaas and members of his team in books such as *Prada*,[3] and also by archi-tectural theorists including Roberto Gargiani.[4] Since 2004, OMA/AMO has also provided sets for Prada's fashion shows and those of its subsidiary Miu Miu in both Milan and Paris, but this aspect of the collaboration remains relatively unexplored.

At the end of 2014, I arranged to meet Ippolito Pestellini Laparelli, an architect and partner at OMA/AMO, at the practice's headquarters in Rotterdam. Pestellini Laparelli worked on fashion shows as a designer for OMA/AMO between 2008 and 2009, and became responsible for the collaboration with Prada in 2011 until he left OMA early in 2020. As partner-in-charge, he had a supervisory role corresponding to that of an art director, overseeing both digital production and stage sets as the collaboration expanded to cover additional typologies. I have continued researching the collaboration between the two companies since, drawing on a variety of sources, including OMA/AMO's in-house archives, and have interviewed many of those involved, from architects and designers to sound artists and photographers. Finally, I have attended numerous Prada shows over the last five years, recording and analysing their content in a systematic fashion.

Existing research on the collaboration between Prada and OMA has largely explored brand communication, and has described the evolution of Prada's retail architecture as a means of 'using architecture as a tool for marketing' while inverting 'the act of consumption, making it a catalyst for communal spaces'.[5] I am more interested in fashion itself – and by fashion I mean the study of dress, adornment and clothing.[6] Obviously, if a fashion house such as Prada needs to come up with new styles several times a year – and in doing so provide glimpses into the future at a micro-scale – it is a machine for generating newness in fashion.

An interview with Markus Schaefer – an architect and founding partner of AMO who was one of the key people in the early stages of the collaboration with Prada – helped to crystallise a fundamental question that I hope to address here and in a

---

2   Mila Ganeva, 'Elegance and Spectacle in Berlin: The Gerson Fashion Store and the Rise of the Modern Fashion Show', in *The Places and Spaces of Fashion, 1800–2007*, ed. John Potvin (New York and London: Routledge, 2009), 127.

3   Rem Koolhaas et al., eds., *Prada* (Milan: Fondazione Prada, 2001).

4   Roberto Gargiani, *Rem Koolhaas/OMA: The Construction of Merveilles*, trans. Stephen Piccolo (Lausanne: EPFL Press, 2008).

5   Anna Klingmann, *Brandscapes: Architecture in the Experience Economy* (Cambridge, Mass.: The MIT Press, 2007), 117.

6   Tim Edwards, *Fashion in Focus: Concepts, Practices and Politics* (Abingdon, Oxon.: Routledge, 2011), 2.

Foreword

related book currently in preparation: how can such newness be generated in an industrialised manner?[7] If we follow the argument proposed by Christophe Van Gerrewey in his book *OMA/Rem Koolhaas: A Critical Reader* that 'The strategy of OMA is to make things architectonically visible – to imagine the immediate future just before it takes place', a fashion show's set is the perfect project to work on.[8] AMO's design processes when developing the concept for a show happen directly alongside Prada's internal design processes for the associated collection. The regularity of these shows – Prada requires at least six different sets per year – and the intensity of design work demand a rigorous method from both architectural practice and fashion house. These microcosms of the future must be created in just eight weeks.

... to a framework ...

It was important to establish a reference system with which to analyse the differing 'future spaces' offered by fashion houses. Most fashion shows are designed by professional production companies, but there have been other interesting collaborations between fashion houses and architectural offices that usually operate within traditional boundaries, such as that between Maison Martin Margiela and Studio Anne Holtrop. Do these collaborations differ in their design processes? And are there contrasts between different fashion cultures, for example between the various so-called fashion capitals?[9]

I began looking for an existing theoretical framework in architectural writing but, as Pestellini Laparelli told me, 'in the architectural world, the fashion shows are disregarded'.[10] Lateral thinking – applying findings from analogous situations in other fields – was required.[11] One interesting approach comes from a German scholar in cultural sciences, Alicia Kühl, who has proposed a compelling conceptual model for positioning, describing and analysing fashion spaces, which I will discuss in the introductory essay that follows, 'Rethinking Fashion Spaces'.

... to a program

Inspired by my research on OMA/AMO's collaboration with Prada, and informed by Kühl's remarkable work, I have developed an alternative conceptual model of fashion spaces with the help of my co-author Kjeld Hansen of the Mobile Technologies Lab here at Kristiania University College in Oslo. Kjeld brought a new perspective to the subject, informed by his research on the interplay between social media, mobile computing and information management in relation to public health and cities. The introductory essay explores the problematics of research and presents our model, which proposes that there are two essential elements to building fashion spaces: an ephemeral architecture, which we term the *site*, and an imagined space facilitated by social media, which we term the *metaspace*.

The second part of the book has been developed with students of the retail design program at the School of Arts, Design, and Media at Kristiania University College, including visiting exchange students. Thanks to our teaching positions and the school's support, Kjeld and I had the opportunity to implement a practice-oriented approach to academic teaching and innovation, and to test our hypotheses in collaboration with students. Our project ran for two semesters in Fall 2018 and Fall 2019. During the first semester, a group of students proposed a thesis for the application of our model of fashion spaces when

7   Markus Schaefer, interview by Vésma Kontere McQuillan, Zurich, 6 February 2017.
8   Christophe Van Gerrewey, ed., *OMA/Rem Koolhaas: A Critical Reader* (Berlin: Birkhauser, 2019), 14.
9   Christopher Breward, *Fashion*, Oxford History of Art (Oxford : Oxford University Press, 2003).
10 Ippolito Pestellini Laparelli, interview by Vésma Kontere McQuillan, Rotterdam, 4 December 2014.
11 Ray Lucas, *Research Methods for Architecture* (London: Laurence King Publishing, 2016), 32.

predicting future trends. A year later, another group produced visual essays illustrating these trends, while continuing research on theoretical perspectives.

The resulting book shows the application of our conceptual model through these visual essays, and explores, researches and defines the fashion space as an emerging area of research within architectural writing. In addition, it has given students valuable practice in collaborating with the international publishing industry, and vital experience of innovation and entrepreneurship.

Sources

- Breward, Christopher. *Fashion*. Oxford History of Art. Oxford: Oxford University Press, 2003.
- Edwards, Tim. *Fashion in Focus: Concepts, Practices and Politics*. Abingdon, Oxon.: Routledge, 2011.
- Ganeva, Mila. 'Elegance and Spectacle in Berlin: The Gerson Fashion Store and the Rise of the Modern Fashion Show'. In *The Places and Spaces of Fashion, 1800–2007*, edited by John Potvin, 121–38. New York and London: Routledge, 2019.
- Gargiani, Roberto. *Rem Koolhaas/OMA: The Construction of Merveilles*. Translated by Stephen Piccolo. Lausanne: EPFL Press, 2008.
- Klingmann, Anna. *Brandscapes: Architecture in the Experience Economy*. Cambridge, Mass.: The MIT Press, 2007.
- Koolhaas, Rem, Jens Hommert, Michael Kubo and Prada, eds. *Prada*. Milan: Fondazione Prada, 2001.
- Lucas, Ray. *Research Methods for Architecture*. London: Laurence King Publishing, 2016.
- Pestellini Laparelli, Ippolito. Interview by Vésma Kontere McQuillan, Rotterdam. 4 December 2014.
- Reichert, Alexander. Interview by Vésma Kontere McQuillan, Basel. 7 February 2017.
- Schaefer, Markus. Interview by Vésma Kontere McQuillan, Zurich. 6 February 2017.
- Van Gerrewey, Christophe, ed. *OMA/Rem Koolhaas: A Critical Reader*. Berlin: Birkhauser, 2019.

Introduction: Rethinking Fashion Spaces

Text
Vésma Kontere McQuillan
& Kjeld Hansen

The fashion show is a creative form of expression. It is artistry and, with its global reach and immediacy in the digital age, it is a platform to communicate attitudes about politics, sexuality, and about religion and family, a place to champion causes and concerns.

Alexandre de Betak[1]

When looking at 25 years of Alexandre de Betak's set designs in Sally Singer's book, *Betak: Fashion Show Revolution*, one cannot help but notice how they act as microcosms of the fashion spaces one finds in the wider world. Within the highly restricted space of a fashion show, it is possible to find answers to serious questions about architecture, society, politics and culture. With this in mind, in this essay we propose a conceptual model of the fashion space that complements existing ideas, concepts and theories. In so doing, we hope to provide an effective model of the contemporary fashion space that defines it as an integrated physical and virtual space.

We argue that there are two essential components of today's fashion spaces. The first is a physical place that has been transformed via ephemeral architecture – for instance a stage set – which we term the *site*. The second is an imagined space that is enabled by the internet and enhanced by social media, which we term the *metaspace*. We start our analysis by drawing on recent architectural thinking, which has promoted greater understandings of the built environment, but we also look at the fields of architectural communication, brand communication, fashion communication and collaborative consumption.

---

1   Alexandre de Betak and Sally Singer, *Betak: Fashion Show Revolution* (London: Phaidon Press, 2017), 7.

Introduction

The current growth in interest around and understanding of fashion spaces is closely connected with the arrival of new means of disseminating and engaging with content, in particular online streaming and social-media platforms. Fashion brands are now able to control their own narrative in both the physical and virtual spheres, and are beginning to forge responsive, or even collaborative, fashion spaces in which the public imagination plays an increasingly important role. These new spaces are starting to contribute to a reimagining of fashion itself, both in terms of the functioning of the industry and of the nature of the product that it sells. In addition, the physical space of fashion shows is now subject to digital mediation, affecting their design and production, and thus significantly altering their role in the creation of fashion spaces.

Our overall objective is to formalise the notion of fashion spaces by proposing a theoretical perspective that provides the necessary tools for future research and analyses. By this means, we aim to help establish the foundations of a common understanding between architecture and fashion, and to provide a language for writing at the intersection of these two disciplines. In particular, we propose a conceptualisation and typology of fashion spaces that we hope can be extended into the spheres of retail design and urbanism.

FASHION AND ARCHITECTURE

Looking at existing literature on architecture and fashion, much has been written on the production of traditional fashion shows, as well as the design of retail spaces. Not many publications, however, focus on the complex integration of the two disciplines in wider urban contexts. *The Geographies of Fashion* by Louise Crewe, a professor of human geography, describes architecture and fashion as two critical aspects in the making of city spaces.[2] She refers in particular to the work of journalist and author

Bradley Quinn, who writes on the space between architecture and fashion. He defines the fashion space as:

[B]oth a written source and a visual representation, read like a text and decoded in cinema-like images. Imbricated with fantasy and desire, as well as suffused with memories and nostalgia for other places, fashion space is always heavily romanticised, and imbued with fiction, fetishism and ideals.[3]

Crewe and Quinn both talk about architecture and fashion as discordant disciplines while discussing their mutuality.[4] They also approach and conceptualise fashion spaces within broader contexts, such as urban form and societal developments.

If one looks at current architectural research, however, it is clear – to paraphrase the French philosopher Gilles Lipovetsky – that the question of fashion is not a fashionable one among architects themselves.[5] While Crewe offers some reflections on why this may be, the fact remains that there are very few examples of architectural writing that seriously discuss the relationship between the two disciplines. One such example is *Architecture, in Fashion*, which grew out of a symposium of the same name held in April 1991 at Princeton University School of Architecture. A collection of essays and projects, the book points out two conflicting correlations between fashion and architecture: on the one hand, architecture is static in comparison with the rapidly changing fashion system; on the other, it deals with clothing

---

2   Louise Crewe, *The Geographies of Fashion: Consumption, Space, and Value* (London: Bloomsbury, 2017), 13.
3   Bradley Quinn, *The Fashion of Architecture* (Oxford: Berg 2003), 35.
4   Crewe 2017, 16.
5   The precise quote is 'The question of fashion is not a fashionable one among intellectuals'. Gilles Lipovetsky, *The Empire of Fashion: Dressing Modern Democracy*, trans. Catherine Porter (Princeton and Oxford: Princeton University Press, 1994), 3.

the body in the same way that fashion does.[6]

In cultural sciences, however, there is some interesting academic work on fashion spaces – and in particular on fashion shows – that relates them to architectural concerns. The German research community has been especially active on the subject, but this poses two challenges: first, German-language publications are less accessible to most researchers than English-language ones; second, linguistic and cultural issues need to be addressed in order to arrive at a common understanding of fashion spaces.

German scholar Alicia Kühl has discussed the topic, presenting formal models of fashion spaces in both German and English. However, there are differences between the framing of her concept in the two languages. In her English-language essay 'Framing "Saints and Sinners"', published in 2014,[7] Kühl writes:

> *By the place of a fashion show I am referring to the* geographical place *where it is held, but one that, based on the 'coloration' it is given in the fashion business, also has social, political, and economic connotations ... The term* location *is used while referring to a concrete point within a place at or in which the fashion show is staged ... The* imaginary space *is the space the designer creates in his/her imagination.*[8]

However, if one reads the original German text of the essay published two years earlier, it becomes clear that there are significant discrepancies between the two versions.[9] For example, the concept of 'place' in the quote above is a translation of the German word *ort*, while 'location' is a translation of *raum*.[10] These translations may be technically correct, but they do not communicate the essence of the German words, or the concepts they embody. Confusingly, *ort* can also be used to mean a location, while *raum* can simply mean a room, or even an infinite space.

Fashion Spaces

In addition, we can detect deeper meanings in Kühl's use of another term, *metaraum*, translated in 'Framing "Saints and Sinners"' as 'imaginary space'.[11] In our view, Kühl's concept of the *metaraum* would be better conveyed in English by an alternative term, metaspace, which is usually defined as a space transcending ordinary physical space. A metaspace is generally understood to be more than just an imaginary space conceived by a single designer, thus it is more appropriate to communicate the wider implications of the German original, *metaraum*. In Kühl's view, this *metaraum*, or metaspace, exists only for the duration of the fashion show. However, we believe that metaspaces can now be made accessible to, shared with and transformed by others through social media, thus increasing their longevity, as we will discuss later.

OMA/AMO, PRADA AND BRANDSCAPES

As it stands, the subject of the fashion space is still characterised by this lack of commonly accepted terminology and concepts, and therefore by a lack of coherence. In order to address this challenge, we first propose to look at the ongoing collaboration between an architectural practice, OMA, and a fashion house, Prada, to consider if it is possible to utilise existing architectural research to help understand the fashion space, and in particular if it is helpful to employ the idea of architecture as a communicative

---

6   Deborah Fausch et al., *Architecture, in Fashion* (New York: Princeton Architectural Press, 1994), 7.
7   Alicia Kühl, 'Framing "Saints and Sinners". Methods of Producing Space in Fashion Shows: Michael Michalsky's Fall/ Winter 2009 Collection', in *Aesthetic Politics in Fashion*, ed. Elke Gaugele (Berlin: Sternberg Press, 2014), 113–29.
8   Kühl 2014, 118.
9   Alicia Kühl, 'Wie Kleidung zu Mode wird Prozesse der Verräumlichung in Modenschauen', in *Räume der Mode*, ed. Gertrud Lehnert (Munich: Wilhelm Fink Verlag, 2012), 57–83.
10   Kühl 2012, 62.
11   Kühl 2014, 118.

medium. We will then move on to ask if it is possible to create a conceptual model to analyse fashion spaces.

OMA, together with its research arm AMO, operates within the traditional boundaries of architecture and urbanism, and has been an important force in the development of new typologies since its founding in 1975.[12] Its co-founder, Rem Koolhaas, is one of the most important names in recent architectural theory, as both writer and practitioner. Among his many areas of interest, he has been exploring the meeting point of architecture and fashion for over 20 years, and it was OMA's long-term collaboration with Prada that introduced the concept of brandscapes, a term coined in the 1980s, into the fashion industry. This concept – the convergence of branding and space in the formation of communication strategies – acted as an important theoretical transition in generating our contemporary notions of fashion spaces.

OMA's application of brandscapes in its projects is discussed in detail in *Brandscapes: Architecture in the Experience Economy* by Anna Klingmann, an OMA team member from 1997 to 2000. She defines the term as the 'branding of architecture', suggesting that it opens up discussion of 'the potential of architecture as a medium to create an identity for people, communities, and places'.[13] Explorations of this potential are frequent in the collaboration between OMA and Prada. For instance, in an associated research portfolio, 'Prada OMA. Work in Progress November 1999. Atlas',[14] there is an unrealised proposal to change the name of a New York metro station to 'Prada' in order to expand Prada's brandscape to encompass the station.

In practice, OMA has created brandscapes for Prada through the continuous repetition of a set of values, images and styles in the fashion shows and architectural projects on which the two firms have collaborated. Koolhaas has defined luxury as 'attention', 'rough', 'intelligence', 'waste' and 'stability'.[15] These values have been consistently communicated through Prada's architectural projects – whether retail spaces, fashion shows or expanded environments – over the last 20 years, but they have also been disseminated through media outlets and other consumer touchpoints.

In its book *Content*, OMA/AMO discusses some of the practice's major projects and activities, including the collaboration with Prada.[16] The publication proposes a future where the purpose of architectural projects is to communicate – as Koolhaas puts it, 'a building was no longer an issue of architecture but of strategy'.[17] Similarly, we might say that the main business of the fashion industry is no longer the production of apparel, but rather the production of content, and of the fashion spaces in which this content resides. Fashion houses can now announce their seasonal collections through the creation of a fashion space that consumers can engage with through social media or a live-stream, influencing the public imagination of the brand and its objects in the process.

TIME AND MEDIA IN FASHION SPACES

Fashion is a dynamic phenomenon. It is required to adapt to rapid changes in political, social, economic and cultural situations. For this reason, it is difficult for a brand to remain relevant and successful all the time. The use of brandscapes tends to involve integrated brand communication, in which all media deliver the same or similar messages, but this is an approach

12 OMA is currently run by eight partners: Rem Koolhaas, Ellen van Loon, Reinier de Graaf, Shohei Shigematsu, Iyad Alsaka, Chris van Duijn, Jason Long and David Gianotten. It maintains offices in Rotterdam, New York, Hong Kong, Beijing, Doha, Dubai and Sydney. https://oma.eu/office.
13 Anna Klingmann, *Brandscapes: Architecture in the Experience Economy* (Cambridge, Mass.: The MIT Press, 2007), 8.
14 The original portfolio is available in the archives of Markus Schaefer. Parts of the portfolio were published in Rem Koolhaas et al., eds., *Prada* (Milan: Fondazione Prada, 2001).994), 3.
15 Markus Schaefer, interview by Vésma Kontere McQuillan, Zurich, 6 February 2017.
16 Rem Koolhaas, ed., *Content* (Cologne: Taschen, 2004).
17 Rem Koolhaas, 'Babylon Falling', in Koolhaas 2004, 118–25.

that can lead to temporary or permanent obsolescence. In the early 2000s, the most successful brandscapes were connected to minimalism, a style perfected by architects such as John Pawson, who developed the spatial aesthetics of Calvin Klein in the United States, and Claudio Silvestrin, who worked with Armani in Milan. Their work was influential at the time, but has now lost much of its relevance, with consequent impacts on the status of the two brands in question.

Time is the critical aspect that differentiates the contemporary fashion space from other spatial and architectural typologies, including brandscapes. On the one hand, fashion spaces can be limited in duration, having often been defined in the past by the length of a fashion show, the impact of a photo shoot, or the existence of a retail space. On the other hand, they may also have an extended life as the expression of a zeitgeist – the spirit of the times, or perhaps the specific look of an era – yet this longevity is essentially retrospective. Today, however, the fashion space is evolving into a vital and ongoing tool in ensuring the continued relevance of brands in a changing marketplace.

In addition, adapting the brand's message to individual media is now critical to the creation of a fashion space. Unlike the integrated communication of the brandscape, not all of the physical places or virtual platforms of the fashion space need to deliver the same message. For example, a brand's Instagram account doesn't have to communicate the same aesthetic as its fashion shows or its stores. The autonomy and sustainability of the contemporary fashion space are linked to its ongoing and flexible engagement with the public imagination around the brand across diverse physical and virtual environments.

There is already a new willingness on the part of brands to recognise and engage with the various expressions of the fashion space, and with their varying durations – from photo shoot, to zeitgeist, to metaspace – as evidenced by the

Fashion Spaces

web-based retail concept introduced by the brand Highsnobiety in 2019:

> *With 15 years' experience of covering product drops, we believe focusing on individual releases instead of following typical retail strategies allows us to highlight the best products, ideas, stories, and talent — regardless of season and trends ... Each drop will be available worldwide, for a limited amount of time, and only while stock lasts. We hope to achieve an entirely new dynamic, rhythm and experience for the highly educated and passionate community that we are a part of and have been crucial in building over the last decade and more.*[18]

Appropriately, the first drop of Highsnobiety's web-based retail concept was Prada Linea Rossa, a sportswear-inspired line for which OMA/AMO and Prada collaborated on several non-architectural projects in the early 2000s, including content production and advertising campaigns.

FRAMING FASHION SPACES: LOCATION, PLACE AND SITE

Informed by Alicia Kühl's work, we have formulated a new conceptualisation of fashion spaces that reflects three technological developments that have profoundly influenced understandings of how these spaces work. First, the rise of Web 2.0 technologies and social-media platforms has provided new opportunities for accessing, sharing and producing content. Second, the development of high-powered smartphones and their seamless

---

18 David Fischer, 'Here Is the Next Chapter in the Story of Highsnobiety', *Highsnobiety*, last modified 12 October 2019, https://www.highsnobiety.com/p/highsnobiety-shopping-platform/.

Introduction

integration into everyday life have made it possible to access and produce information anywhere, at any time. Thirdly, sophisticated infrastructure, including high-speed mobile internet and cloud computing, has made highly visual content, such as images and videos, an integrated part of our daily information flow. In this context, we propose to define the key concepts of the fashion space – location, place and site – as follows:

Location

Location is often defined as a place, but it is perhaps better understood as a precise position, such as the grid reference on a map, or a GPS (Global Positioning System) coordinate. Mobile interfaces have helped to change the ways that we perceive a location, in part because of the new possibilities they offer for attaching information to material, including an exact coordinate. For example, it is possible to 'geo-tag' photographs to a precise position on a virtual map using GPS coordinates, or to 'tag' a post on a social-media platform to any business, building or institution that has a virtual profile, as well as to individuals. In both instances, a library of information is built up about that location, including users' engagement with and appropriation of the location.[19] Thus, for the purposes of our conceptualisation of fashion spaces, we define the term *location* as referring to the coordinates of a real-world geographic position.

Place

In contrast to the concrete notion of location outlined above, we define *place* as the abstract idea that exists around a location. According to Elizabeth Parsons, Pauline Maclaran and Andreas Chatzidakis, there are four components that characterise the identity of a place: (1) the physical setting and its physical contents; (2) the social, political and economic connotations that create the context of the physical setting; (3) the activities and events produced inside the place; and (4) the individual and collective meanings created through the intentions and experiences that are related to the place.[20] Combining this with Tom Porter's definition of the term in an architectural context – 'the site for a building is a place in the making'[21] – we could say that, in fashion, the abstracted place provides the context for the creation of a site.

Site

In his 2009 essay 'Inserting Fashion into Space', John Potvin explores the nature of sites by saying that 'sites can be marked out as places and spaces which define and are transformed through, by and because of the subjects and objects of fashion'.[22] Understanding the nature of a location, and its status as an abstracted place, is key to understanding its potential as a site for fashion. In this vein, Tom Porter, in *Archispeak: An Illustrated Guide to Architectural Terms*, states that 'site appraisal is often the first tangible information produced at the onset of the design process'. It not only represents a moment of analysis of the context for a building proposal, but also 'provides a major stimulus for initial thoughts on the development of an architectural form, and thus of a site'.[23]

There are three major ways through which brands choose or are allocated venues that provide a potential site for a fashion show, and these ways inform the resulting fashion spaces in turn. The first is to use one offered to them by the organiser of a fashion week, a strategy often utilised by younger

19   Adriana de Souza e Silva and Jordan Frith, *Mobile Interfaces in Public Spaces: Locational Privacy, Control, and Urban Sociability* (New York: Routledge, 2012).

20   Elizabeth Parsons, Pauline Maclaran and Andreas Chatzidakis, *Contemporary Issues in Marketing and Consumer Behaviour*, 2nd ed. (Abingdon, Oxon.: Routledge, 2018).

21   Tom Porter, *Archispeak: An Illustrated Guide to Architectural Terms* (London and New York: Spon Press, 2004), 142.

22   John Potvin, 'Introduction: Inserting Fashion into Space', in *The Places and Spaces of Fashion, 1800–2007*, ed. John Potvin (New York: Routledge, 2009), 9.

23   Porter 2004, 171–72.

and less established fashion designers. The second is to hand-pick the potential place for a site, and then reuse it each season, a strategy preferred by most established fashion houses. For example, Prada showed at via Fogazzaro 36 in Milan continuously from 2000 to 2018. Such continuous use of venues can transform their meaning as sites in a fashion context. Some are even chosen because their original typology or function opposes the idea of fashion. For example, the French Communist Party Headquarters in Paris, designed by Brazilian architect Oscar Niemeyer and completed in 1980, is now known and marketed as a venue for events and fashion shows.

The third strategy is to choose a potential site according to the designer's vision for a particular season, reinforcing the idea behind the collection. For instance, since its debut in 2014, Vetements has used post-Soviet aesthetics to present its alternative street fashion, and held its shows in locations and places that are foreign to the world of commercial fashion – a gay club, a Chinese restaurant, a church or the underpass of a ring road. By bringing high fashion to unusual locations and places, including those where countercultures flourish, the brand experiments with and evolves their potential as sites.

Perhaps pertinent to this interpretation is a call from the architecture journal *OASE* for abstracts: 'In architecture, the site is "merely" the context for the object to be designed; in urbanism and landscape architecture, (the transformation of) the site is the subject of design itself.'[24] We propose that, in fashion spaces, the site is both the context for the object to be designed, and also the design of that object.

FRAMING FASHION SPACES: METASPACES

In her discussion of *metaraum* (or, as we have translated it here, metaspace[25]), Alicia Kühl defines it in opposition to her concepts of place and location:

[Metaspace] cannot be localised, as it is abstract. It is a not-yet-realised, imagined space, the initial place, or an idea of a place. The 'metaspace' becomes a place in the process of spatialisation during the performance of a fashion show, but it disappears after 15 minutes, when the fashion show is over.[26]

According to Kühl, once the show ends, the metaspace 'exists only in a reduced form, as an essence in the visitor's memory'.[27] As discussed, this may well have been accurate in 2012, when she published the original article, but the rise of social-media platforms has altered the situation fundamentally. In the age of Instagram, the significance and longevity of the metaspace have both radically increased, and its existence is increasingly palpable. Fashion is now mediated and communicated through private, semi-private and commercial accounts on social-media sites. As a result, fashion today inhabits a metaspace on a permanent basis. And, thanks to features such as Instagram Shopping, the distance between virtual metaspace and physical purchase is now very small – today, the metaspace functions as an expanded retail space.[28]

CONCLUSION

For a long time, a fashion space was a temporary but culturally significant space anchored in the location, place and site of the

24 'Call for Abstracts OASE#107', *OASE*, 21 November 2019, https://www.oasejournal.nl/en/ Issues.

25 In this instance, 'metaspace' is our translation of Kühl's *metaraum*, since her essay was published only in German.

26 Kühl 2012, 62.

27 Kühl 2012, 63.

28 Josh Constine, 'Instagram Launches Shopping Checkout, Charging Sellers a Fee', *TechCrunch*, 19 March 2019, https://techcrunch.com/2019/03/19/instagram-checkout/.

fashion show – a space in which architecture and fashion came together to create an ephemeral metaspace. Now, the location, place and site continue to provide the physical setting of the fashion show, but the fashion show itself is only a part of the fashion space, which can exist both before and after the show itself. During the fashion show, we experience a brief co-occurrence of the location, site, place and metaspace to form one fashion space. Yet this is only the point of departure for an enduring metaspace, which lives on in our imagination and re-imagination after the curtain closes, through social media and other co-creation practices. In this way, the fashion space endures.

Sources

- Betak, Alexandre de, and Sally Singer. *Betak: Fashion Show Revolution*. London: Phaidon Press, 2017.
- Crewe, Louise. *The Geographies of Fashion: Consumption, Space, and Value*. London: Bloomsbury, 2017.
- Constine, Josh. 'Instagram Launches Shopping Checkout, Charging Sellers a Fee'. *TechCrunch*. 19 March 2019. https://techcrunch.com/2019/03/19/instagram-checkout.
- Fausch, Deborah, Paulette Singley, Rodolphe El-Khoury and Zvi Efrat. *Architecture, in Fashion*. New York: Princeton Architectural Press, 1994.
- Fischer, David. 'Here Is the Next Chapter in the Story of Highsnobiety'. *Highsnobiety*. Last modified 1 May 2019. https://www.highsnobiety.com/p/highsnobiety-shopping-platform.
- Klingmann, Anna. *Brandscapes: Architecture in the Experience Economy*. Cambridge, Mass.: The MIT Press, 2007.
- Koolhaas, Rem, Jens Hommert, Michael Kubo and Prada, eds. *Prada*. Milan: Fondazione Prada, 2001.
- Koolhaas, Rem, ed. *Content*. Cologne: Taschen, 2004.
- Kühl, Alicia. 'Framing "Saints and Sinners". Methods of Producing Space in Fashion Shows: Michael Michalsky's Fall/Winter 2009 Collection'. In *Aesthetic Politics in Fashion*, edited by Elke Gaugele, 113–29. Berlin: Sternberg Press, 2014.
- Kühl, Alicia. 'Wie Kleidung zu Mode wird Prozesse der Verräumlichung in Modenschauen'. In *Räume der Mode*, edited by Gertrud Lehnert, 57–83. Munich: Wilhelm Fink Verlag, 2012.
- Lipovetsky, Gilles. *The Empire of Fashion: Dressing Modern Democracy*, translated by Catherine Porter. Princeton and Oxford: Princeton University Press, 1994.
- OASE Foundation. 'Call for Abstracts OASE#107'. *OASE*. 21 November 2019. https://www.oasejournal.nl/en/Issues.
- Parsons, Elizabeth, Pauline Maclaran and Andreas Chatzidakis. *Contemporary Issues in Marketing and Consumer Behaviour*. 2nd ed. Abingdon, Oxon.: Routledge, 2018.
- Porter, Tom. *Archispeak: An Illustrated Guide to Architectural Terms*. London and New York: Spon Press, 2004.
- Potvin, John. 'Introduction: Inserting Fashion into Spaces'. In *The Places and Spaces of Fashion, 1800–2007*, edited by John Potvin, 1–15. New York: Routledge, 2009.
- Quinn, Bradley. *The Fashion of Architecture*. Oxford: Berg, 2003.
- Schaefer, Markus. Interview by Vésma Kontere McQuillan, Zurich. 6 February 2017.
- Silva, Adriana de Souza e, and Jordan Frith. *Mobile Interfaces in Public Spaces: Locational Privacy, Control, and Urban Sociability*. New York: Routledge, 2012.

Introduction

Fashion Spaces in Practice: Prada S/S 2021

Text
Vésma Kontere McQuillan

Visuals
Courtesy of Prada

On 24 September 2020, Prada's Spring/Summer 2021 womenswear show was streamed on the brand's Instagram feed. The video was not a live-stream, but a pre-taped presentation taking the form of a montage, recorded without spectators present. For the show's physical environment, OMA/AMO created a simple square space in shades of yellow, cut off from the larger room beyond by wall-to-ceiling curtains in the manner of a TV studio. Its only decorations – six chandelier-like clusters of monitors and cameras – hosted all the necessary technology. In contrast to the label's Spring/Summer 2021 menswear show, where screens showed films by respected artists, here the screens simply showed the number of the look and the names of the models. These names were also incorporated into the soundtrack composed by British-Canadian electronic musician Richie Hawtin under his Plastikman alias. The models were all newcomers to fashion shows, and their vulnerability provided additional emotional intensity to an event conceived of as an examination of the dialogue between humans and machines.

Thanks to OMA/AMO's past spatial experiments, the catwalk had already started to lose its role as the main compositional principle of Prada's fashion spaces well before the COVID-19 pandemic. However, for the digital presentation of new collections, there is now no need for a catwalk at all. When our theoretical model for fashion spaces was conceived, the physical show remained dominant. Yet its framework can still be applied to this new breed of digital fashion show, helping us evaluate which aspects of the model are getting weaker, and which are becoming more potent, while also facilitating a greater understanding of the collection being presented. In the case of Prada's Spring/Summer 2021 womenswear show, the *location* (via Lorenzini 14, Milan) and the *place* (Fondazione Prada) were no longer important. Instead, the key to achieving a long-lasting *metaspace* lay in the design of the *site*, for which OMA/AMO utilised the typology of the TV studio rather than that of the fashion set, neatly capturing the spirit of our times, in which we watch endless screens in our pursuit of human connection.

Fashion Spaces

Fashion Spaces in Practice

Fashion Spaces

Fashion Spaces in Practice

Fashion Spaces

FATOU

Fashion Spaces in Practice

Fashion Spaces in Practice: Gosha Rubchinskiy F/W 2017

Text
Vésma Kontere McQuillan

Visuals
Courtesy of Gosha Rubchinskiy

It is possible for a designer's creativity and a brand's strategy – along with wider economic and social trends – to influence all four components of a fashion space: location, place, site and metaspace. To take one example, Russian fashion designer Gosha Rubchinskiy presented his Fall/Winter 2017 collection in a specific *location* on the south bank of the Pregolya River in Kaliningrad: the old Stock Exchange, built in the 19th century when the city was part of Prussia and known as Königsberg. The building was partially destroyed during the Second World War, and the city was then annexed by the Soviet Union. Afterwards, the shell of the Stock Exchange was used as a backdrop for war films, before being restored in the 1960s to become a maritime centre and a regional centre for youth culture. It has recently been refurbished to house the city's Museum of Fine Arts. As a result, it has rich and diverse meanings as a *place*. Given the complex and contentious histories of both Kaliningrad and the Stock Exchange, this was not a traditional location or place for a fashion brand. Rubchinskiy's decision to utilise this context in the creation of a *site*, offering a football-inspired spin on post-Soviet chic, reflected his strategy for creating a *metaspace* that engages the collection's target audience – youths who do not consider themselves part of the establishment. This choice of location, place, site and metaspace exemplifies the prevailing trend of importing street fashion into the luxury-fashion sector.

Fashion Spaces in Practice

Fashion Spaces

Fashion Spaces in Practice

Fashion Spaces in Practice

Fashion Spaces

Fashion Spaces in Practice

Fashion Spaces

Let's Meet in Metaspace: Introducing Student Case Studies

Text
Vésma Kontere McQuillan
& Kjeld Hansen

Visuals
Daniel Jørgensen
& Ingrid Herstad

The age of social media has brought a new type of space into the world of fashion. During traditional fashion shows, architecture and fashion merge, creating ephemeral spaces for the presentation of new collections. Today, these spaces can survive in the digital sphere, to be shared, re-shared and commented on via social media. Fashion spaces have moved from being anchored in space and time, to existing as co-created, ever-changing and vital metaspaces, where the dialogue between designers, consumers and industry leaders continues well after the show has ended.

These changes were precipitated by the second digitalisation wave in 2005, when Web 2.0 applications brought about crucial shifts in the behaviour patterns of consumers, with far-reaching consequences.[1] Before, metaspaces had lived on mainly in physical objects and individual memories; now they moved to the digital realm and co-creative experiences. As a result, new conceptual models for fashion spaces were urgently required, and new questions about their nature needed to be asked. For instance, could they have a greater impact than that offered by the physical experience of a fashion show? Has their introduction, and the resulting discourse, influenced the design of physical retail spaces? And how can designers use these new spaces as opportunities for innovative cultural and commercial production?

The case studies that follow utilise the conceptual model of the contemporary fashion space proposed in this book's introductory essay. Each discusses a location, defining it as both a site and a place, before exploring its transformation into a metaspace through various social-media strategies. Each includes a visual project that explores the implications of this transformation. The authors are students at Kristiania University College in Oslo, which

---

1   Philipp Teufel and Rainer Zimmermann, *Holistic Retail Design: Reshaping Shopping for the Digital Era* (Amsterdam: Frame Publishers, 2015), 6.

Let's Meet in Metaspace

is one of the fastest growing capitals in Europe. The expansion of the city's economy and tech sector make it a particularly interesting subject when analysing the changing nature of fashion spaces. Between them, the case studies cast light on the past, present and future of fashion spaces, helping us to address many of the questions raised in the introductory essay. Most importantly, they suggest how the fashion industry might respond to the major social, political, economic and cultural changes currently taking place across the world.

Previously, fashion spaces were closely connected to specific locations, thus the first case study, 'Life after Lagerfeld', explores the classic approach to staging fashion shows through the example of the French fashion house Chanel, the heritage of which is wrapped up in that of Paris, the city of haute couture. It proposes that, just as the formative role played by haute couture in the fashion industry is currently being challenged by streetwear and athleisure gear, the role of location in fashion spaces is now being questioned by new manifestations of the metaspace.

The second case study, 'Streaming the Extreme', highlights the disruption being inflicted on the fashion industry by the internet, including the fraying of the link between fashion spaces and physical spaces. It tells the story of Alexander McQueen's last collection, 'Plato's Atlantis', which was shown in Paris in October 2009. Preceded by a tweet from Lady Gaga, this was the first live-streamed fashion show, and introduced social media's critical role in transforming the fashion show's metaspace from an ephemeral construct to an enduring one.

'Keeping Up with Changes' explores the disruption of the fashion industry at the hands of newcomers from other creative industries such as music and television. In particular, it examines the pioneering role of Kanye West, whose Yeezy collaborations have caused a shift in understandings of location in the fashion industry. Among West's many innovations, his use of tropes drawn from reality TV in order to reconceive the runway for social media has proved hugely influential. Fashion shows no longer need to exist in the traditional sense – due to West's intervention, the fashion space as we know it today was born, with its metaspace newly expanded, and much of it relocated to social media. The success of this strategy is, however, highly dependent on the skill with which social-media campaigns are conceived and executed.

The fourth case study, 'Curating German Fashion', applies the methods introduced by West, and reviews the strategic use of fashion spaces by brands wishing to establish a presence in a new location. Now that the traditional fashion capitals are losing their power, cities such as Oslo have the potential to gain increased significance as fashion spaces, with major implications for international fashion. The evolving nature of fashion spaces is investigated, along with the new opportunities that are now available for both emerging brands and up-and-coming locations.

The next case study, 'Championing Consignment Retail', takes the form of a conversation with the owners of Oslo's first streetwear consignment store, Ditto, and looks at the practicalities of establishing and running one of the new breed of fashion spaces. This portrait of an existing store, and of the Gen Z entrepreneurs behind its concept, also informs the case study that follows, 'From Streets to Fashion Spaces'. This proposes the strategic reframing of a skatepark in Majorstuen, Oslo, to create a fashion runway, and explores how this might alter an established urban space while also creating a new fashion space. This temporary transformation could challenge the public perception and imagination of a local asset, and also of the fashion brand presented there.

Finally, 'Moving Beyond Gendered Spaces' brings us to the future of fashion spaces, examining what might happen when location, place and site have all lost much of their significance as the role of the metaspace grows. The authors conclude that gender-neutral retail could exist independently of location, place and site, shaping the collective imagination and departing from existing norms of gendered space. It's clear from this case study that a new generation is now taking control of and expanding discussions around gender and its relation to architecture.

According to the architect and literary theorist Christophe Van Gerrewey, recent architectural discourse has been 'split between a not so much contemporary but rather simultaneous reception and reproduction online, and an academic industry that has, in an ongoing process of scientification and rationalisation, drained both contemporary architecture as a subject as well as the critical distinction between good and bad options.'[2] We strongly believe that a new generation of designers has the power to change this situation, and that academic research within spatial-design studies must inspire innovations in design work, both in terms of aesthetics and technology. Our motivation behind defining, describing and analysing fashion spaces is to learn how to create architecture that offers co-creative experiences that involve both designers and consumers. We invite the reader to dive into our experiments in rethinking fashion spaces within academia and praxis.

Sources

- Teufel, Philipp, and Rainer Zimmermann. *Holistic Retail Design: Reshaping Shopping for the Digital Era*. Amsterdam: Frame Publishers, 2015.
- Van Gerrewey, Christophe, ed. *OMA/Rem Koolhaas: A Critical Reader*. Berlin: Birkhauser, 2019.

2   Christophe Van Gerrewey, ed., *OMA/Rem Koolhaas: A Critical Reader* (Berlin: Birkhauser, 2019), 17.

LOCATION OF STUDENT CASE STUDIES

Oslo, Norway

Paris, France

Chicago, USA

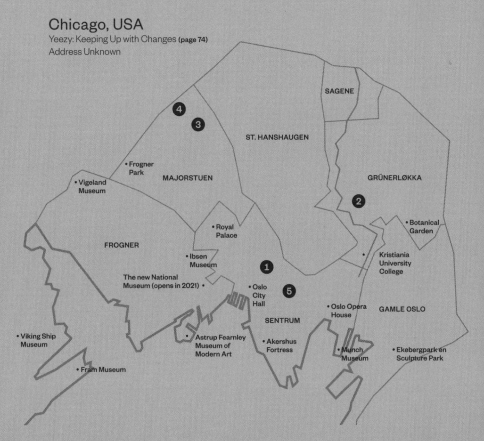

Chanel: Life after Lagerfeld

Text
Tina Therese Rustadstuen
& Mareike de Boer

Visuals
Tina Therese Rustadstuen

THE LEGACY OF COCO CHANEL

One of Gabrielle 'Coco' Chanel's main contributions to fashion was attaining a dominant position in what was still a man's world. In a related achievement, she was also the first designer to introduce traditional menswear items, such as trousers, into the wardrobes of fashionable women. She started a rebellion in fashion, and is still cited by many as an inspiration, embodying freedom, passion and style. Karl Lagerfeld, the charismatic creative director at Chanel from 1983 to 2019, was careful to perpetuate her spirit.

For many people, the Chanel brand, with its powerful story, has become a way of life. The popular perception of the brand is still anchored in the tweed suit, flap bag, little black dress and N°5 perfume.[1] These are legendary fashion pieces, or 'cult objects', and they help to promote all of Chanel's activities, and to broadcast a clear brand image across the world.

Among Chanel's strengths is its use of traditional linear storytelling when staging fashion shows, referencing the brand's heritage and emphasising the trickle-down theory of fashion, in which styles flow vertically from the upper classes to the rest of society – this is perhaps the oldest model of the diffusion of fashion.[2] In order to leverage this heritage, Chanel's shows often employ aesthetic ideas drawn from the early 20th century, when Coco Chanel first revolutionised fashion. This choice ensures that everyone immediately understands and relates to the story that the brand wishes to tell. During his time at Chanel, Lagerfeld took total control over the customer's imagination in his staging of shows – the metaspace he created was absolutely defined,

---

1   Carola Anna Elias and Vittoria von Gizycki, eds., *Omnichannel Branding: Digitalisierung als Basis erlebnis- und beziehungsorientierter Markenführung* (Wiesbaden: Springer Gabler, 2008), 309.

2   Kim Eundeok, Ann Marie Fiore and Hyejeong Kim, *Fashion Trends: Analysis and Forecasting* (New York: Berg, 2011).

Fashion Spaces

leaving no room for misinterpretation. In this way, he ensured that his ideas were conveyed in a powerful fashion, and that customers would purchase products once they left the venue.

THE GRAND PALAIS

Since 2006, Chanel has held its shows in the Grand Palais, Paris, a building that Lagerfeld discovered as a child.[3] It was originally built for the Exposition Universelle held in 1900, and is now used as a cultural venue – it was designated a historic monument by the French Ministry of Culture in 2000. Chanel's president of fashion, Bruno Pavlovsky, once said that the building is 'much more than a simple monument in the heart of Paris. Its remarkable architecture makes it a true source of inspiration and creation for Karl Lagerfeld.'[4]

A good example of the role played by the Grand Palais in the Chanel brand is the Spring/Summer 2019 show. In the early 20th century, wealthy Parisians spent their holidays at resorts on the French coast, thus the decision was taken to create a beach within the Grand Palais – a building from the same era – recalling the activities of the leisured classes, and drawing on the brand's illustrious heritage. The resulting fashion space told a unified story of Chanel and of its connections with Paris through the significance of the chosen location, place and site.

Chanel often relies on such strong storytelling to promote its brand image – the decision to build the concept for this fashion show entirely around the beach necessitated the construction of a complex set, yet the result communicated a simple, straightforward idea in a highly effective manner.

---

3   'Fashion Parades', Grandpalais.fr, 18 January 2012, https://www.grandpalais.fr/de/node/4727.
4   Chloe Street, 'Chanel Commits 25 Million Euros to Renovate the Grand Palais in Paris', *Evening Standard*, 13 February 2018, https://www.standard.co.uk/fashion/chanel-commits-25-million-euros-to-renovation-of-pariss-grand-palais-a3765371.html.

Chanel's customers tend to come from the upper-middle or upper classes, thus the beach theme, with its associations of luxury and exclusivity, reached the entire spectrum of this target group. Through such stagings, Chanel presents itself as a brand that epitomises tradition and elegance, and the show's concept lingers in viewers' minds long afterwards. By repeatedly holding its shows in the same place, the Grand Palais, the associations between the location and the brand are reinforced.

The linear nature of Chanel's narratives is mirrored in coverage of its fashion shows online, for instance in the social-media accounts of such journalists as Tim Blanks of *The Business of Fashion*. When discussing the Spring/Summer 2019 show, Blanks described the design processes employed to create its metaspace, for instance talking about the use of 'real people and real water'.[5] Such coverage demonstrates that Lagerfeld's strict conception of the show's metaspace helps to ensure that it is perpetuated on social media.

THE COCO CHANEL SUITE, GRAND HOTEL OSLO

Inspired by Chanel's use of linear narrative in the staging of its fashion shows, we created a fictional hotel suite that Coco Chanel might have occupied if she had spent her life in Oslo rather than Paris. The idea came from the fact that Chanel lived at the same hotel, the Ritz Paris, for 34 years – the hotel still rents out her rooms as 'The Coco Chanel Suite' today. The design of our proposed suite, located in the Grand Hotel Oslo on Karl Johans gate, is based on Chanel's 'cult objects', for

---

5   Tim Blanks (@timblanks), 'The Lifeguard is real. So is the water. And the audience. Everything else is a grand illusion. It's the world according to Karl', *Instagram*, 2 October 2018, https://www.instagram.com/p/BobLKzVn50Y/.

Chanel: Life after Lagerfeld

Fashion Spaces

instance its N°5 perfume. This way, we used metaspace to define the site in Oslo, far away from the brand's traditional location, in Paris.

CONCLUSION

The loss of Chanel's acclaimed creative director, Karl Lagerfeld, who defined the brand for more than 35 years, offers the fashion house an opportunity to re-examine how it creates its fashion spaces. As we have discussed, Chanel's strategy around its fashion spaces has been to define the metaspace very precisely, and thereby control the narrative that surrounds its fashion objects and shows. When taking the brand forward, we suggest that a new creative director might continue to exploit its heritage, but also consider the need to promote Chanel to new consumer groups by exploring other possibilities offered by the fashion space model. By imagining how Coco Chanel might have lived her life in Oslo, we wanted to explore how fashion operates in the metaspace, pay tribute to the genius of Karl Lagerfeld, and also suggest how a closer relationship could be built between the Chanel brand and its customers by adopting a freer interpretation of metaspace.

Sources

- Blanks, Tim (@timblanks). 'The lifeguard is real. So is the water. And the audience. Everything else is a grand illusion. It's the world according to Karl'. *Instagram*, 2 October 2018. https://www.instagram.com/p/BobLKzVn50Y/.
- Elias, Carola Anna and Vittoria von Gizycki, eds. *Omnichannel Branding: Digitalisierung als Basis erlebnis- und beziehungsorientierter Markenführung*. Wiesbaden: Springer Gabler, 2008.
- Eundeok, Kim, Ann Marie Fiore and Hyejeong Kim. *Fashion Trends: Analysis and Forecasting*. New York: Berg, 2011.
- Réunion des Musées Nationaux – Grand Palais. 'Fashion Parades'. Grandpalais.fr, 18 January 2012. https://www.grandpalais.fr/de/node/4727.
- Street, Chloe. 'Chanel Commits 25 Million Euros to Renovate the Grand Palais in Paris'. *Evening Standard*, 13 February 2018. https://www.standard.co.uk/fashion/chanel-commits-25-million-euros-to-renovation-of-pariss-grand-palais-a3765371.html.

Alexander McQueen: Streaming the Extreme

Text
Ingrid Herstad &
Elise Aurora Kjæran Pedersen

Visuals
Ingrid Herstad

THE LIFE OF ALEXANDER MCQUEEN

Aged 16, Lee Alexander McQueen gained an apprenticeship at Anderson & Sheppard, Savile Row, London, tailors by appointment to the British royal family. He went on to study fashion design at London's Central Saint Martins College of Art and Design, graduating in 1992 and founding his own label that same year. His Fall/Winter 1995 show, 'Highland Rape', made his name, and led to his appointment as head designer for Givenchy, following in the footsteps of John Galliano. Unfortunately, McQueen felt that his creativity was limited at Givenchy so quit after five years, but his work there brought international recognition and resulted in a partnership with the Gucci Group that took his own eponymous brand to a global audience.[1]

McQueen was a pioneer in his approach to fashion shows and his creation of innovative metaspaces, always remaining a step ahead of the rest of the industry. He felt that it was essential that his shows should have an emotional impact, and embraced new methods and technology in order to achieve this, stating, 'There is no way back for me now. I am going to take you on journeys you've never dreamed were possible.'[2] To achieve this, he planned his shows before he even started on the clothes.[3] 'He could never design a collection without knowing what the show was,' according to Sam Gainsbury who, together with Anna Whiting, produced many of McQueen's shows.[4]

McQueen's Spring/Summer 1999 show, 'No. 13', explored the possibility that technology might supplant craft. For its finale, the former ballerina Shalom Harlow appeared wearing a white paper dress. Two robots then proceeded to spray both

---

1   Andrew Bolton, *Alexander McQueen: Savage Beauty* (New Haven, Conn.: Yale University Press, 2011).
2   Bolton 2011, 184.
3   Bolton 2011.
4   Bolton 2011, 24.

Fashion Spaces

her and the dress in neon-yellow and black paints. The show had a lasting impact throughout the industry, in part due to its experimental character – it succeeded in being both disturbing and serene. McQueen's Spring/Summer 2001 show, 'Voss', was similarly conceptual, challenging the audience to question what it considered beautiful and what it saw as grotesque. For the final set piece, the journalist Michelle Olley lay naked on a couch, her curves in stark contrast to the thin, angular bodies of the models around her – as McQueen put it, 'These beautiful models were walking around in the room, and then suddenly this woman who wouldn't be considered beautiful was revealed.' [5] Olley breathed through an oxygen tube, in a reference to a famous photograph by Joel-Peter Witkins, *Sanitarium* (1983).

'Voss' indicates how important it was for McQueen to make his audience conscious of their own thoughts and perceptions and, like 'No. 13', is a good example of a fashion show in which the metaspace created by the designer had an influence that outlasted even that of the clothes on display.[6] We can only guess at the reasons why McQueen did things so differently from other designers, but he certainly put his whole being into his vocation, stating in the catalogue of his 2011 exhibition at the Metropolitan Museum of Art, New York: 'What you see in the work is the person himself. And my heart is in my work.'[7]

'PLATO'S ATLANTIS'

In his last show before his death, 'Plato's Atlantis', at which his Spring/Summer 2010 collection was presented, McQueen merged Charles Darwin's theory of evolution with growing concerns around global warming, postulating that humans would

---

5   Bolton 2011, 142.
6   Bolton 2011.
7   Bolton 2011, 12.

Fashion Spaces

need to evolve into ocean creatures to survive. Its most important legacy was that it was the first fashion show live-streamed on the internet, an achievement given a huge publicity boost by Lady Gaga, who tweeted the link just before showtime alongside the announcement that she would premiere a new song on the runway. According to Emma Hope Alwood in *Dazed*, it was the 'McQueen show that changed the future of fashion … giving outsiders a glimpse into its previously hidden inner workings.'[8]

This trailblazing approach is now used, and even expanded upon, by most major fashion houses. For example, at her 2016 show during New York Fashion Week, Carolina Herrera partnered up with the platform Livestream to install two 360-degree cameras at the venue, giving internet users the freedom to move around and choose their own viewing angles, garnering a great deal of attention for the brand. Similarly, Louis Vuitton collaborated with Snapchat for its Cruise 2020 womenswear show in New York, for which they created a handbag entitled 'The Canvas of the Future'. Everyone attending was given a special code that they could use to unlock the augmented-reality handbag and play with it during and after the show.[9] Live-streaming has changed our idea of fashion spaces forever, and that's why we decided to focus on this technology for our proposal.

'IN MEMORIAM ALEXANDER MCQUEEN' SPRING/SUMMER 2021

How would Alexander McQueen stage a fashion show if he were alive today? We decided to try and answer this question, choosing the Stade Pierre de Coubertin in Paris as the place for this hypothetical show, in part because of its size, but also because it offers the possibility of achieving total darkness. The catwalk could go along the sides of the court, with the inner part hidden by curtains resembling those used in in theatres.

At first, the event would seem like a regular fashion show, with the models walking along the black marble runway that circles the court. When they return to the runway after all the outfits have been shown, the models stand still and the lights are switched off. When they are switched back on, the models are lying 'dead' on the floor, and the curtains behind have risen, revealing a burning forest. This disturbing scenario reflects McQueen's embrace of controversy, but it is also indeterminate, because the viewer does not immediately understand that the models are dead. And, finally, it is relevant for the times we live in, as it addresses the climate crisis.

In addition, the show would be streamed on Instagram. When the lights are turned back on at the Stade Pierre de Coubertin, and the curtains are raised to reveal the burning forest, an AR (augmented-reality) filter of flames is added to this live-stream, transforming the experience of the show for its online viewers, and symbolising the death of fashion.

CONCLUSION

By including an AR filter on the live-stream, we would create the opportunity for two different metaspaces to exist simultaneously, one at the site, the other online. The narratives are the same, but the explicit depiction of fire online makes the message less ambiguous and thus less likely to be misunderstood by the online audience. All of the show's viewers would enjoy the exclusivity of being present at the Stade Pierre de Coubertin, but those attending in person do not experience

---

8   Emma Hope Allwood, 'The McQueen Show that Changed the Future of Fashion', *Dazed*, 2 August 2016, https://www.dazeddigital.com/fashion/article/32285/1/the-mcqueen-show-that-changed-the-future-of-fashion-platos-atlantis-nick-knight.

9   Jessica Schiffer, 'How to Turn a Fashion Show into an Online "Moment"', *Vogue Business*, 9 September 2019, https://www.voguebusiness.com/fashion/fashion-shows-social-media-moment-instagram-gucci-louis-vuitton.

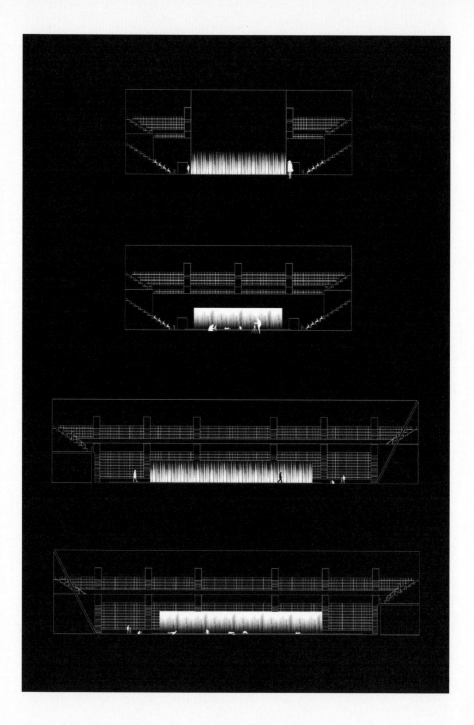

Fashion Spaces

the onscreen fire, while those watching the live-stream cannot experience the show's narrative without it. You can't get it all – both alternatives afford a different impression. As a result, two metaspaces have been created for one show.

The act of 'burning down' the live-stream, which seems to destroy the online metaspace, might strike one as extreme if it weren't for the precedents provided by McQueen throughout his career. He was looking for extreme reactions – it was his creative method.[10] Our proposal reflects the ongoing development of fashion spaces since his death. The first metaspace takes place in Paris, and utilises the established rules of the traditional fashion show; the second metaspace destroys itself on Instagram, reflecting McQueen's own passing.

Sources

- Allwood, Emma Hope. 'The McQueen Show that Changed the Future of Fashion'. *Dazed*, 2 August 2016. https://www.dazeddigital.com/fashion/article/32285/1/the-mcqueen-show-that-changed-the-future-of-fashion-platos-atlantis-nick-knight.
- Bolton, Andrew. *Alexander McQueen: Savage Beauty.* New Haven, Conn.: Yale University Press, 2011.
- Schiffer, Jessica. 'How to Turn a Fashion Show into an Online "Moment"'. *Vogue Business*, 9 September 2019. https://www.voguebusiness.com/fashion/fashion-shows-social-media-moment-instagram-gucci-louis-vuitton.

10 Bolton 2011, 12.

Yeezy: Keeping Up with Changes

Text
Dawt Tha Tawk &
Maren Bardine Lindseth

Visuals
Dawt Tha Tawk

THE CHANGING FASHION WORLD

The fashion world is undergoing a rapid transformation. Fashion weeks, as we currently know them, were developed nearly a century ago by American retailers to increase sales. Newspapers, fashion magazines and other print media started to report on these shows to cater to rising public interest. Since then, it has become the norm to film and broadcast fashion shows as documentaries and news items – and also, in the last decade, to disseminate them through live-streams. It is clear that smartphones and social media are increasingly influencing the directions that the fashion industry is taking. They have become seamlessly integrated into our everyday lives, changing how we interact with each other and with our surroundings.

Today, fashion bloggers and social influencers attract large audiences and can play the sorts of roles in the industry that newspapers and magazines used to play. Fashion houses are, to various degrees, using social media as a tool for creating awareness and forging interaction with consumers. For many brands, fashion shows are now designed to impress not only the audience watching in the venue, but also those viewing and interacting on social media.

Fashion shows are still considered by many to be the main forum for presenting new creations and ideas. The industry's calendar is meticulously organised around the biannual fashion shows in New York, London, Milan and Paris, which are carefully scheduled to avoid drawing attention away from each other. Attendance is by invitation only, ensuring an exclusive audience that is dominated by members of the press, buyers and celebrities. However, fashion bloggers and influencers have recently joined their ranks, and now make up a significant section of those present. In addition, many emerging brands are highly adept in using social media, and are devising fresh ways of presenting fashion that radically break away from existing norms. In this essay, we will discuss how the fashion brand

Fashion Spaces

Yeezy broke the prevailing rules surrounding fashion shows and succeeded in creating a new fashion space.

YEEZY SEASON 6

In September 2017, Yeezy was lined up to present its latest collection during New York Fashion Week, but cancelled shortly beforehand. Instead, the brand opted to show its collection three months later in Los Angeles, utilising an entirely new format. Its founder, the rap star-turned-designer Kanye West, decided to take advantage of his celebrity status, and his sizable social-media following, to launch the Yeezy Season 6 collection on the sidewalks of Calabasas, Los Angeles, without any prior warning. He used only one model, his wife Kim Kardashian West – a huge reality-TV star and social-media celebrity in her own right – to showcase the collection. She modelled 16 different outfits, and the entire event was photographed by the paparazzi who constantly follow the couple. These photographs were then printed in magazines and shared on social media, and Kim Kardashian West posted the pictures on her Twitter and Instagram accounts.

Yeezy accomplished two major innovations with this display in Calabasas. First, it effectively broke with the established norm that fashion brands present their latest collection in a certain location at a certain time, for instance at New York Fashion Week. Kanye West and Kim Kardashian West both command enormous interest throughout the year, both in traditional media and on social media, thus are not reliant on the additional interest that a fashion week attracts. Secondly, Yeezy broke decisively with the tradition that a fashion show is an exclusive event at which the sole attendees are 'by invitation only' guests. Instead, social-media followers of Kim Kardashian West were given the opportunity to feel that they themselves were invited to an improvised fashion show. The pictures of her

Fashion Spaces

Yeezy: Keeping Up with Changes

wearing the new collection had their own highly relatable narrative, since they were taken on an ordinary sidewalk. Through its novel approach, Yeezy forged new relations with its customers and brought about a change in perceptions of the fashion show in the public imagination.

The unusual presentation of the Yeezy Season 6 collection created an immediate internet buzz, and when the hype peaked, the brand released the entire collection for pre-order on its website.[1] This approach drew on other aspects of Yeezy's social-media strategy, for instance its posts capturing Kim Kardashian West in everyday situations, such as having a coffee break or running errands, while wearing the brand's products. The overwhelming interest caused established fashion brands to take notice. Prada, for instance, developed and arguably finetuned Yeezy's approach in events such as the launch of the Prada Linea Rossa Fall/Winter 2019 collection, for which Willow Smith wore items from the collection while navigating London's subway system. The event had a spontaneous air, and was shared live on Prada's Instagram account. The posts featured the so-called 'Shop Now' button, making it possible for users to purchase items immediately.[2]

KANYE TAKES CHICAGO

We were fascinated by the way in which Yeezy successfully challenged the norms of the fashion industry by changing when and where a fashion collection can be presented, and in particular by its adoption of mundane settings for its narratives. We wanted to explore this concept by introducing another unexpected element into the traditional fashion system – an unconventional location. Kanye West grew up in Chicago, which is not a city that is considered important within the fashion industry. Moving the presentation of the next Yeezy collection to West's hometown would come as a surprise to the brand's community.

In Chicago, we would create the first branded retail space for Yeezy, consisting of a gallery, a pop-up store for new collections, and a permanent store for smaller products and collaborations with emerging and established artists. We conceive this as an imaginary space with no precise address. The central idea is to involve local communities by exploring and enhancing their creativity and their voice. West is known for being controversial and shocking, and we believe the store would attract attention not just because of its unconventional location but also because it would create a new relationship between the brand and its customers. In this regard, the concept of bringing Yeezy to West's hometown seems meaningful on both a personal level and a strategic level.

CONCLUSION

The presentation of Yeezy Season 6 questioned the ideas that a fashion collection needs to be introduced at a certain location at a certain time, and that it needs to be presented to a select audience. Instead, Yeezy chose a location and time of its own preference, and an audience with which it already had a relationship. In *Fashion Forecasting*, Evelyn Brannon and Lorynn Divita write about the 'strategic window', defining it as the right time to launch an innovation.[3] For most fashion brands, New York Fashion Week would be considered one such window, but Yeezy consistently rejects the fashion world's rules. Kanye West and Kim Kardashian West can command media attention

---

1   Steff Yotka, 'Can Yeezy's See-Now-Buy-Now Paparazzi Proposition Work for Other Fashion Brands?', *Vogue*, 11 December 2017, https://www.vogue.com/article/yeezy-season-6-papparazzi-release.
2   Vésma Kontere McQuillan (@vesma_k_mcquillan), '@yeezymafia method in praxis', *Instagram*, 7 October 2019, https://www.instagram.com/p/B3Uru1KCA6-/.
3   Evelyn L. Brannon and Lorynn Divita, *Fashion Forecasting*, 4th ed. (New York: Fairchild Books, 2015), 2.

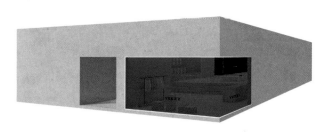

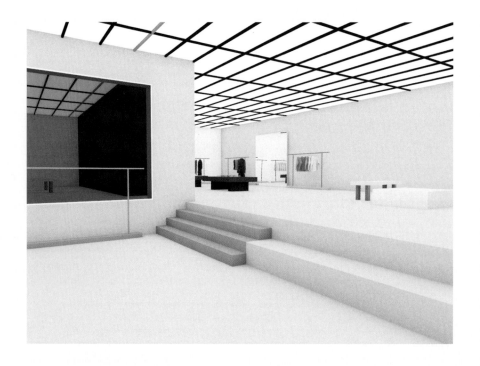

Fashion Spaces

throughout the year, thus Yeezy's strategic window is significantly bigger than that provided by traditional fashion weeks – the combination of the surprise cancellation of the New York launch and West's high profile on social media proved irresistible, and bypassed the need for a conventional fashion show. Furthermore, Yeezy managed to influence how fashion is imagined and reimagined – the metaspace – both during and after the presentation, leveraging the massive interest in and documentation of the collection on social media.

Sources

- Brannon, Evelyn L. and Lorynn Divita. *Fashion Forecasting*, 4th ed. New York: Fairchild Books, 2015.
- McQuillan, Vésma Kontere (@vesma_k_mcquillan). '@yeezymafia method in praxis'. *Instagram*, 7 October 2019. https://www.instagram.com/p/B3Uru1KCA6-/.
- Yotka, Steff. 'Can Yeezy's See-Now-Buy-Now Paparazzi Proposition Work for Other Fashion Brands?'. *Vogue*, 11 December 2017. https://www.vogue.com/article/yeezy-season-6-papparazzi-release.

Not Just Berlin: Curating German Fashion

Text
Katharina Brinkmann &
Maren Bardine Lindseth

Visuals
Katharina Brinkmann

CHANGING PERCEPTIONS OF GERMAN FASHION

Our project, Not Just Berlin, adopts a pop-up retail strategy while giving us an opportunity to curate a selection of independent German fashion designers. It consists of two parts: an Instagram account, @notjust_berlin, and a proposal for a pop-up store in Oslo.

In the past, there have been many prejudices about German style and fashion – in particular, both are often characterised as conservative, difficult and overly modest.[1] One of the most famous German fashion designers is Jil Sander, who pioneered minimalistic fashion trends in the 1980s and still receives significant recognition for her current collections. However, younger designers are breaking away from such purism, embracing diverse cultural influences to create collections that are vivid, colourful and eclectic. As a result, this is a good moment to change long-standing perceptions of German fashion, using Instagram to help in this process.

@NOTJUST_BERLIN

We have set up an Instagram account, @notjust_berlin, that highlights a number of inspirational German fashion designers. It might be expected that a significant majority would come from Berlin, but in fact many come from Munich, Hamburg or cities in the western state of North Rhine-Westphalia. The purpose of our account is to inspire visitors through the work of these designers, and to create a new metaspace for German fashion. Finally, we hope to support the designers themselves and make them better known. To provide a backstory for each designer, our posts always include architecture from their hometowns.

---

1   Marcel Berndt, 'Warum es vielen Deutschen an Stil fehlt', *WirtschaftsWoche*, 6 February 2015, https://www.wiwo.de/erfolg/trends/fragwuerdige-mode-warum-es-vielen-deutschen-an-stil-fehlt/11115198.html.

Fashion Spaces

RETAIL ON INSTAGRAM

According to recent research, 'a third of all Instagram users have now bought an item of clothing they saw on the social network'.[2] Certainly, the purchasing of products on Instagram is easier than it has ever been. Brands can now tag items to indicate which are available, and these products can then be bought using the application, thus brands do not even need an online shop to make sales.[3] Additionally, the customer is saved the effort of going to a store, whether virtual or physical, and searching for items. For most brands, it remains important to have their own website, thus the 'product stickers' on Instagram posts can still link to an online shop. But does this mean that brands no longer need a physical store?

CURATED INSTAGRAM FEEDS

Many emerging brands now establish themselves through their use of Instagram, employing the platform as a 'curated feed'.[4] One of the pioneers of these 'Instagram-famous' brands was Lisa Bühler, who started out curating an Instagram feed consisting of posts on fashion, interior design and, occasionally, retro films.[5] The account became a big success, allowing Bühler to launch her own fashion label in 2015, Lisa Says Gah, which is based in San Francisco. She began to release her collections via posts on Instagram that show customers or ordinary people wearing her clothing in seemingly random everyday situations. Today, Lisa Says Gah also stocks a number of other independent designers, for example the Copenhagen-based brand Ganni. Around the

---

2   Leah Harper, 'Squaring Up: How Insta-fashion Is Changing the Way We Shop', *The Guardian*, 31 March 2019, https://www.theguardian.com/fashion/2019/mar/31/squaring-up-how-instagram-fashion-is-changing-the-way-we-shop.
3   Harper 2019.
4   Harper 2019.
5   Harper 2019.

same time as Bühler's success with Lisa Says Gah, the beauty brand Glossier was also achieving fame through Instagram, spinning off from the successful blog *Into The Gloss* by Glossier's founder Emily Weiss. Today, Glossier is still using Instagram as its main marketing tool.[6]

Alongside its online presence, Lisa Says Gah has a store in San Francisco stocking the designers featured on its Instagram posts. Even for these Instagram-famous brands, it is often helpful to have a physical store in which to sell products, as it allows them to attract a larger clientele, and also engage with those who prefer to get to know a brand and its products in real life, and who may not even be on Instagram.

These brands have understood the key advantages of Instagram and put them to use. Perhaps the most important of these is that the platform is easily accessible, thus has become 'the best discovery tool for customers in fashion', according to Ditte Reffstrup, creative director at Ganni.[7] Traditional fashion shows are connected to one location, but brands using Instagram – and their online audiences – have no need to be tied down in this manner. Ultimately, fashion is no longer chained to locations – it just needs to reach those who are using social media to find inspiration.

For many, Instagram feels like a natural place to encounter a person, a brand or even a lifestyle, thus fashion posts can seem like a personal recommendation from a friend.[8] As a result, Instagram provides a fantastic opportunity for everyone – and especially independent designers – to reach out and inspire those who share the same aesthetic and style. The success of many emerging brands has been enhanced by this sense of authenticity and intimacy. In addition, a new breed of 'curators' has emerged on Instagram, who are perceived 'as being design-conscious arbiters of style or cool sophistication', according to the artist and curator Adrian George. The upshot is that many new fashion trends have emerged out of the platform.[9]

NOT JUST BERLIN POP-UP STORE

For the second part of our Not Just Berlin project, we developed a proposal for a pop-up store that would provide a hub specifically dedicated to German fashion brands. However, we required a location with specific characteristics for this venture. It needed to be outside Germany, so that the brands it stocked would be removed from their usual environment, and thus seem new and exclusive. For similar reasons, it made sense to avoid the locations of the four main fashion shows: Paris, New York, Milan and London. However, we felt that the store should be in a European city, as understandings of fashion tend to be relatively similar across Europe, making it easier to attract an audience.

Our decision fell on Oslo, as it met these criteria. Our pop-up store would be located in Grünerløkka, a trendy area known for alternative lifestyles that has numerous small residential and retail spaces, thus is perfect for a store with a two-month lifespan. As mentioned, the four major fashion centres in Germany are Berlin, Munich, Hamburg and North Rhine-Westphalia, so we designed four sections for the store, each with a different look that referenced one of these locations. Customers would be able to identify which 'city' they were in as they move through the store, thus would gain an understanding of the designers' backgrounds, just as they would on the @notjust_berlin Instagram feed. In order to always be presenting something new, the designers featured in the store would change every three or four weeks. The store would function as a showcase for the designers, allowing customers to look at, touch and try on the garments, and stocking a limited range

6 Kat Boogard, 'Glossier Marketing Decoded: How to Instagram Like Glossier', *Sked Social*, 19 March 2019, https://skedsocial.com/blog/glossier-marketing-strategy-social-media/.
7 Harper 2019.
8 Harper 2019.
9 Adrian George, *The Curator's Handbook* (London: Thames & Hudson, 2015), 12.

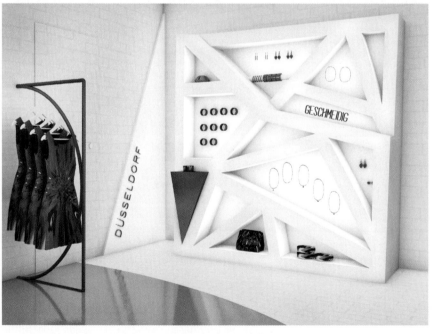

Fashion Spaces

Not Just Berlin: Curating German Fashion

ΛREΛ 1:MUNICH

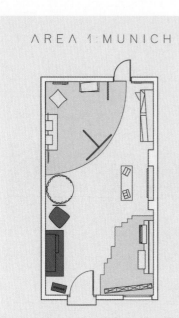

ΛREΛ 2:BERLIN

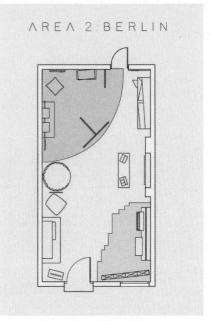

ΛREΛ 3:NRW

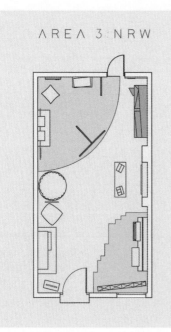

ΛREΛ 4:HAMBURG

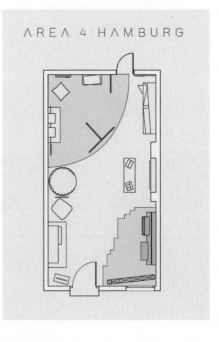

Fashion Spaces

of products for immediate purchase. In addition, customers at the store would be able to order any piece from the full collection with the help of a sales assistant, and the items would then be delivered directly to their homes.

CONCLUSION

Ultimately, the social-media approach to retail and branding has already fundamentally changed our understanding of fashion. Instagram makes it possible to make a brand – and its apparel – accessible and appealing to all, transcending borders and rendering locations irrelevant. Once Instagram users across Europe, or perhaps even worldwide, can become aware of a fashion label or designer through the platform, it will no longer be so important for the brand to have a physical store in its home country. Social media has also changed the metaspace. This can now be created not just during a fashion show, but also while surfing the web – in this case, while exploring a curated selection of German fashion on Instagram. Finally, social media, if used strategically, provides an incredible opportunity for smaller brands and lesser-known designers to increase their profile – in particular, it can open new doors for niche labels such as SET by Maya Junger and Lala Berlin, both of which are featured on the @notjust_berlin Instagram feed.

Sources

- Berndt, Marcel. 'Warum es vielen Deutschen an Stil fehlt'. *WirtschaftsWoche*, 6 February 2015. https://www.wiwo.de/erfolg/trends/fragwuerdige-mode-warum-es-vielen-deutschen-an-stil-fehlt/11115198.html.
- Boogard, Kat. 'Glossier Marketing Decoded: How to Instagram Like Glossier'. *Sked Social*, 19 March 2019. https://skedsocial.com/blog/glossier-marketing-strategy-social-media/.
- George, Adrian. *The Curator's Handbook*. London: Thames & Hudson, 2015.
- Harper, Leah. 'Squaring Up: How Insta-fashion Is Changing the Way We Shop'. *The Guardian*, 31 March 2019. https://www.theguardian.com/fashion/2019/mar/31/squaring-up-how-instagram-fashion-is-changing-the-way-we-shop.

Ditto: Championing Consignment Retail

Text
Iiro Piipponen

Visuals
Iiro Piipponen

FROM POP-UP TO PERMANENCE

The story of Ditto starts with a trip taken by one of its founders, Salar Bahador, to Los Angeles in 2016. While there, he visited Round Two, one of the first buy-sell-trade stores in the city, and decided to establish a similar store back home in Oslo. He then got in touch with three friends – Bror Neby Hilland, Anders Eriksen Knagenhjelm and Didrik Dahr Nygaard – and together they set up Ditto.

Ditto is a startup that offers the chance for anyone interested in consignment retail to get involved. The founders have created a collective, and invite those doing things that they find interesting – music, photography, almost anything – to join Ditto and work on projects together through co-creation practices. These can take place in physical space, online, or both.

Ditto launched in 2017 with a pop-up store near Oslo's main shopping street, Bogstadveien. The project only lasted a week, but created a lot of interest, so in September 2019 Ditto opened its first permanent bricks-and-mortar store on a side street in Majorstuen. The neighbourhood is dominated by big retail chains, so rental costs are high – it is not a place where you find many alternative or youth-oriented businesses. Not only is Ditto's location unusual, its hours are different from those of its larger neighbours – the store is open from Thursday to Saturday only, and from noon to six o'clock in the evening.

I met with Didrik Dahr Nyggard and Solvår Levi Øyen, who joined the team after the initial pop-up, to find out more about Ditto and its value system. We also spoke about how to build a community interested in sustainable fashion, and the processes that go on behind the scenes in the retail sector.

How do you guys know each other?

SOLVÅR: Three of the founders went to school together, right?

DIDRIK: No, only me and Bror [Neby Hilland]. We've known

each other since first grade, actually. Bror was the one who really made us all come together. He brought me and Anders [Eriksen Knagenhjelm] in.

SOLVÅR: And me too – we went to school together later.

DIDRIK: He's really the link that brought us all together. He was the one who said, 'Let's do this ... Let's try to make this work.' He also designed the Ditto logo – he's had a big impact on the visual identity.

Are you all the same age?

SOLVÅR: Yeah, pretty much, we're all in our early 20s.

Why did you choose the name 'Ditto'?

DIDRIK: In Norwegian and English, 'ditto' means something like 'same here'. It was used a lot by our parents' generation in the 1980s and 1990s. We thought that it was a cool word for this concept because we refer a lot to the styles of that era.

You started as a pop-up, right?

DIDRIK: Yes – finding the first location was the most difficult part. Collecting clothes and getting funding was okay in comparison. When you're a new firm or a new concept, no one really takes you seriously, because you have nothing to show. You just have this big idea, but people don't tend to believe in you.

I happened to walk past an empty space in Bogstadveien and saw a phone number in the window. I called it and told the woman who picked up the phone about our concept, and that I wanted to rent the space for a week, nothing permanent. I didn't

feel that I was being taken seriously because she said, 'Yeah, I'll send you a mail and see what we can do.' I could tell she wasn't interested so I searched for her on the internet and found where she worked. Then I went to her office and asked to see her, and ended up waiting for quite a long time. Finally, she gave me five minutes in between meetings. I made it clear to her just how passionate I was about my idea, and how I really wanted it to work out. I think that was the point when she started to take me seriously.

Why did you decide to open a permanent store?

SOLVÅR: Testing the market and building the brand was a long journey. It had always been the goal to open a permanent shop, but if we'd opened one two years earlier, before anyone knew about us, the first weeks would have been so much harder. It would have been much more work if we'd had to do the marketing at the same time as stocking and running the store. We needed to establish the brand, but also introduce this new retail concept, which is only now starting to become better known. We wanted to check out if it was possible to do this kind of thing in Oslo. And we've discovered that it is, absolutely.

DIDRIK: It was also important to see if we could make it work economically. After our pop-ups, we saw that the idea had potential, but it's kind of hard to make a decent profit with pop-ups because there are so many things you need to open the store that you don't need after-wards – it involves a lot of investment for just that short period. When you invest in a permanent store, you can recover those costs over time.

SOLVÅR: The nice thing about pop-ups is that you can

approach the experience just as you would the production of an advertisement or a movie. You make it happen, and then you're done. With a permanent shop, it's continuous and you can't stop. You can't just walk away. You have to keep it open; you have to have new clothes every single week. And, instead of the single intense burst of overtime before a pop-up opens, now it never ends. But it's our third week and so far the response has been so great. We're really happy we decided to do this.

Did you have some specific reason to open the shop in Majorstuen?

SOLVÅR: It was crucial to find a place that was within our budget – retail spaces are really expensive in Oslo. It couldn't be too far away from where people shop, but also not too close so that the rent wasn't too high – it was a balancing act. We searched all summer in 2019, looking at different parts of Oslo that might work for this particular concept. Our initial thought was Grünerløkka because there's a lot of similar stores – vintage, second-hand, independent. We felt we would fit in really well in that environment, and we have some friends who opened a store there a year ago, Good Vibes Vintage, and it's gone really well for them.

But then we reconsidered our approach, and thought perhaps we could reach just as many people, or even more, if we went somewhere we're not competing with everyone. It was a little bit random that we actually ended up here in Majorstuen, but it was the best location that cropped up at the time – it's close to Bogstadveien, and there aren't many competitors in the independent sector.

Ditto: Championing Consignment Retail

Fashion Spaces

Ditto: Championing Consignment Retail

When we found this space, it finally all became possible – it was like, 'OK, now we're good, now we can do it.' We were still worried that there might not be that many people just randomly stopping by the store, but there are!

Did you renovate all of this by yourselves?

DIDRIK: Yes. It was a huge job, so much bigger than we thought it would be. We started out with huge ambitions – that's pretty typical for us, we always have big dreams – but we didn't understand quite how hard it would be to reach our goal and how much work it would take. There are seven of us, we know about clothes, and we know a little bit about how to run a business. But we know nothing at all about renovation and remodelling, despite which we decided to remove a wall that divided the space in two.

Fortunately, we had some really great help – Bror's stepfather has worked as a contractor, and he'd built shops for other people before, so he helped us a lot. We also had my uncle and aunt who work at Snøhetta, one of the most famous architecture firms in Norway – they knew how to design and how to build, and how the whole process works. They showed us how to do things technically, but they didn't have time to actually sit here and tear down the wall, or fix the windows and the floor.

SOLVÅR: They told us what to do, which materials to use, and the most efficient methods. And then they said, 'Go ahead and try it.' So we did, and sometimes it worked really well, and at other times we needed to do it over and over again. For example, originally there was a really nice parquet floor.

DIDRIK: Well, looking back, it was really nice.

SOLVÅR: We should have kept it. We could see that underneath the parquet there were some original tiles and we thought, if we tore up the floor, we could uncover those. So we took up the parquet, and then we took up the tatty linoleum beneath, which was a really horrible process, but when we got down to the original tiles they were in a pretty bad condition. We decided to make the best of the situation, switching out some of the worst tiles. When we finished, it didn't look that great, but the second we put in the clothes and mirrors and lamps and all that, it went together perfectly. Now I think it's cool, it's a really nice touch, but it was definitely one of the biggest jobs – apart from taking down the wall. We had to change many of the windows too because they were broken or covered in paint.

DIDRIK: Now, sitting in the store, it feels like you're outside – it feels like an extension of the street – but it didn't feel that way before, because all the top windows were covered in green or black paint. Changing those was one of the best things we did – it makes the space so much lighter, and so much more comfortable. And we did everything ourselves. What I really like about Ditto is that it's fun to start a business where you learn so much along the way. You don't have a huge budget, and you don't have that much funding, so you have to do things yourself. You have to find alternative solutions. You have to take the harder road. It's a lot of work, and it takes a lot of energy, and sometimes you feel, 'Oh my God, why did we tear up this floor? Why the hell did we decide to do this? Why are we opening a store?' But, after all that, you learn so much.

Fashion Spaces

Ditto: Championing Consignment Retail

Fashion Spaces

SOLVÅR: You get that extreme feeling of ownership. That's so
         important to us – the fact that we can say we actu-
         ally made this store from the ground up makes it
         even more our own. Those three weeks were maybe
         the hardest three weeks that I've ever had, but it was
         really, really worth it.

How do you source all the clothes?

DIDRIK: Our customers come in with them. People in Norway
         have so many clothes they don't use – insane
         amounts. Ask any Norwegian person and they will
         tell you, 'Most of the space in my wardrobe is filled
         with clothes I never wear.' All of the garments you
         can see here, or most of them, are from people
         coming into the shop and saying, 'I never use this,
         I want to sell it.' Then we decide a price and buy it,
         or alternatively put it on a consignment deal, so the
         customer gets money when the item is sold. Some
         clothes we know will definitely sell; some clothes we
         like but we don't know if they will sell, or if they will
         sell for the price we put on them. If something that
         we've taken on consignment doesn't sell, we give it
         back or we reduce the price.
                  That was one of the biggest risks, as we
         hadn't tried this system before. For our pop-ups,
         we purchased clothes from friends, or from friends of
         friends. We bought a lot of vintage items online as well.
         But we knew that, if we stuck to those sources, we
         weren't always going to be able to find all the clothes
         that we needed to sell each week for Ditto to work. But
         the consignment approach is going really well. People
         come in with clothes all the time – quite often we have
         to say no. They could sell their clothes online instead,

Ditto: Championing Consignment Retail

but it's a lot more work. You have to meet the buyers; they have to try on the garment at your home or you have to send it to them; and you have to follow up on conversations constantly. But if you come to Ditto, you can just make the sale, and then you're done. I think that really appeals to a lot of people, just being able to bring in a bag of clothes they don't use anymore – then we can look at it, and maybe buy them.

SOLVÅR: And that's another of the main benefits. You can actually go to a specific location and try clothing on. Lots of the clothes that you buy online, especially the rare ones, you never know if they'll fit or not, as some of the sizes are a bit odd. We wanted to set up a store where we have all those rare items, and you can actually come in and try them and see for yourself.

How do you decide what you want to sell? Are there particular brands that you're looking for?

SOLVÅR: There are, of course, always some brands that are more popular than others. From a market perspective, we take that into account, but the brands have to fit our identity as well. That even goes for the 'hype brands'. Some have a bad reputation for one reason or another – the environment, racism, homophobia and so on – so we won't take them in as we don't want to support them. Vintage stuff tends to be easier. And we handpick everything. There are seven of us, so we don't always agree on what's cool and what's not, but we try to compromise.

DIDRIK: Some stores take in anything from brands that sell, such as Supreme, or Off-White, or Palace. And a lot of it will sell, just because it's that brand. But we don't want to take in clothes on that basis. It can be a plus that the brand sells well, but we would rather take in clothes that fit with the store's identity. We want to be different from everyone else and have our own personality, and it's important that this shows through in the clothes we sell.

SOLVÅR: The fact that we spend so much time handpicking and researching the brands, and have so many discussions within our team – what fits and what we should steer clear of – is definitely what makes Ditto special.

DIDRIK: It's important that we would wear these clothes ourselves – that these are styles we support. If you were wearing any of the clothes we sell here, and we happened to see you in the street, we would think, 'That looks cool.'

Could you mention some of the main brands you like?

SOLVÅR: We do have quite a lot of Supreme, which is a hyped brand, but I feel we take in a good balance of standard brands and some that are more specialist. We also have Palace, which is not as hyped as Supreme. It's a bit more niche, but they have a lot of really cool pieces. Then of course we have The North Face, some Patagonia, Stone Island, Bape and Vlone. And some vintage Dolce & Gabbana Sport too – we're trying to get more of that because we like the aesthetics, but it's very expensive, and we don't yet know if we'll be able to buy and sell it successfully.

Another thing is that the clothes need to be in good condition – we want to sell clothes that will last for a long time, not be ruined in the first wash. Fortunately, a lot of the brands we've mentioned do actually make high-quality clothes.

Fashion Spaces

Ditto: Championing Consignment Retail

You suggested that you don't take in some brands because of their reputation. Can you say any more about that?

SOLVÅR: We constantly discuss brands within the team – do we support this brand? Does it fit with our aesthetic? Does it have a good reputation? Does it respect the environment and its workers? Are there any other ethical considerations? Is it a brand that we really want in our store? And of course there are some brands that we don't want because of their declining market value – for instance shoes by Yeezy are now dropping in price. Or it can be aesthetics – we have an ongoing discussion about whether or not we should take Anti Social Social Club. Some of us like it, others don't.

What are your main marketing channels?

DIDRIK: Instagram – we use Instagram a lot. We explored the idea of being more active on other social media, for instance Facebook and Snapchat, but there's really no point. Through Instagram, we get everything that we need. We have lots of followers – people who come in the shop always have Instagram, and they follow us. Through Instagram we can reach the people that we need to reach, and we can promote ourselves in the way that we want. It really fits our needs.

SOLVÅR: We have a lot of freedom on Instagram. We can make a portfolio that represents our brand and our concept really well. We have complete control over how we use it, how pictures look, how videos are edited, the stories we put out and all that. We don't feel that we're reaching the people that we really want to through Facebook – it's still useful for creating events, but then we use Instagram to spread the word about those events.

Do you make all the content yourselves?

SOLVÅR: We do. We spend a lot of time and money planning and creating the content. As well as running the shop, we have a lot of other projects that we're working on – doing extra projects is always so much fun. Collecting clothes for shoots, finding locations, scouting for models and coming up with ideas are all such collaborative processes. We work with lots of photographers we want to support, and they want to support our work too – creative people can come and help us, we can help them, and we can work together. And the end result is content that we can use on our channels, and they can use on their channels too. In that way, we share everything. I think it is one of the coolest aspects of Ditto that we use so many young creatives and we produce so many cool things.

Who is your typical customer?

DIDRIK: They range from 14 to 35. I feel that it is often younger customers who buy the hype items and other pricier items – there's a lot of interest in those sorts of categories from customers aged between 14 and 17, maybe even younger. We don't have many who are over 35, simply because the styles we stock aren't really for those generations.

SOLVÅR: We market across that age range. We usually say that Ditto is a place for people who like fashion, and that could basically be anyone because we have

Ditto: Championing Consignment Retail

such a large range of styles, brands and prices. It's actually a pretty big target group.

Why are people interested in buying clothes from Ditto?

SOLVÅR: I think customers like the fact that we've travelled to so many places to find stuff, and not just in Norway. People also want to buy clothes here because they know that they'll find brands that are popular, or trending, or hyped. And they can shop for second-hand or vintage pieces. That is so important to young people right now – these days, you can get really cool pieces of used clothing, so you don't have to buy new stuff all the time. Fast fashion is a major problem for the clothing industry. It's one of the biggest of all environmental problems, unfortunately.

What sets Ditto apart from the other vintage and second-hand shops?

DIDRIK: The whole environmental thing is a big motivator for us – there's so much fast fashion nowadays. You buy something one week, and then it's like, 'Oh, this week, it's not cool anymore, throw it out.' So much fashion is so cheap – it's a dirty industry. According to recent studies, ten per cent of environmental damage is caused by the clothing industry, maybe even fifteen per cent. It's crazy.

We want to promote the fact that our approach helps limit the environmental impact of fashion. And a big part of that approach is not just about reselling second-hand clothes, but also the idea that you should buy good-quality clothes, and actually use them. And then, if you don't like a garment anymore, or if you want to renew your wardrobe, you can still sell it, because it's a well-made piece of clothing. Shopping becomes more of a community thing. These clothes go from person to person, and everyone can feel like they have a new piece of clothing – even though it's not new, it can be new to you.

SOLVÅR: This is such a big part of our concept – we know that a lot of these clothes are not ethically produced, but we still want to make sure that their lives are extended. And we also know that many of the fabrics in this shop are not good for the environment, but to make sure that the clothes are resold and last a bit longer is really important to us.

DIDRIK: We also produce some clothes ourselves, made by a guy we know here in Norway. He buys quality textiles – last time the fabric came from Italy – and then he makes the clothes himself. In the long term, our dream is to bring together ethical producers in the local community and like-minded consumers.

How do you see the future of Ditto?

DIDRIK: I'm not really sure to be honest. I don't know where we will be a year from now. I don't know if we'll change all that much to be honest, as long as we like the clothes, as long as we like where it's going. It just depends really. Maybe we'll concentrate on making more of our own stuff, maybe we'll move away from streetwear.

SOLVÅR: We're going to carry on in our own way, with a shop that stocks clothes that we like. It doesn't have to be streetwear. We've stocked some really weird, indefinable clothes – is this street style, or is it some archaic fashion? Sometimes we don't know. I hope we continue doing side projects and producing lots of content – we're getting really good at it. Some of us want to expand Ditto into the nightlife scene, perhaps turning it into a club concept. And maybe we'll make something on the radio one day, who knows? It really is up to us and our imaginations.

DIDRIK: The most important thing is that we can stand behind everything we do.

From the Street to Fashion Spaces

Text
Maren Bjelland &
Vilde Aurora Johannessen

Visuals
Maren Bjelland

THE RISE OF STREET STYLE

Designers are constantly thinking about how their brands can innovate, and how to increase their relevance. One answer is to pay close attention to local markets, and make references to their norms and cultures. In this case study, we will take a look at the evolution of streetwear and how, in only a handful of years, it has become one of the most important trends in the fashion industry. We will also consider why streetwear resonates so strongly in Norway, and how it echoes an important aspect of the country's preferred style of dress, which tends to reflect the national passion for active living and the great outdoors. Using these ideas, we will explore the implications of repurposing a skatepark in Majorstuen, Oslo, as a fashion space, with the aim of integrating the megatrends of a streetwear brand with local culture. Our intention is to use the authenticity and familiarity of the skatepark to generate openness and curiosity in Oslo for fashion shows in general, and street style in particular.

WHEN STREETWEAR EMERGED FROM THE STREETS

It might be difficult to imagine that streetwear first emerged as a subculture, given that it is now so dominant in the fashion world. Even long-established brands, such as Balenciaga and Prada, are now incorporating elements into their collections and shows. So how did streetwear become so important to so many fashion brands, and what kind of relevance does it bring to them?[1]

Streetwear emerged from 1970s skate culture in California, and the term 'street style' was soon applied to both

---

1   Jian DeLeon, 'How Hip-Hop Left a Lasting Influence on Streetwear and Fashion', *Highsnobiety*, 2 October 2018, https://www.highsnobiety.com/p/hip-hop-streetwear-fashion-influence/.

skateboarders' clothes and wider skate culture.[2] In the 1970s, many different American subcultures impacted each other, especially in big cities such as New York, where people of different backgrounds and cultures met and found inspiration in one another's lifestyles. This process led to new influences and directions in fashion.[3] In the 1980s, street style found its way to New York just as hip-hop culture was developing in the Bronx. Streetwear's baggy, loose clothing was perfectly suited to the technical dance moves that characterised hip-hop at the time, such as head spins, popping and locking.[4] During the 1990s and early 2000s, streetwear developed into the style that we know today, while the establishment of dedicated brands such as Supreme commercialised and communicated the culture to a much wider audience.[5]

The merging of the cultures of street style and hip-hop is still evident today. Hip-hop artists such as Run-DMC, who released the pioneering song 'My Adidas' in 1986, and more recently Pharrell Williams, with his love for Japanese street-style brand A Bathing Ape, continue to be very influential in the development of streetwear and its brands. However, one rapper has proved to be more significant than any other in shaping and commercialising today's street-style brands: Kanye West. His successful collaboration with Adidas on the brand Yeezy has shown that hip-hop artists, and in particular rappers, are still the most important force in the development of street-style fashion.[6]

2   'The History of Streetstyle', Icoolkid.com, 6 October 2019, https://www.icoolkid.com/article/history-streetwear.

3   Evelyn L. Brannon and Lorynn Divita, Fashion Forecasting, 4th ed. (New York: Fairchild Books, 2015), 118.

4   DeLeon 2018.

5   Jo Kwok Yee Lee, 'Would Streetwear Really Be as Popular Without Hip Hop?', Streetwear Jobs, 20 September 2018, https://streetwearjobs.com/history-of-streetwear-hiphop/.

6   Tom Banham, 'The Story of Hip-Hop Style, from Run DMC to ASAP Rocky', Fashionbeans, 6 October 2019, https://www.fashionbeans.com/article/hip-hop-style/#.

Fashion Spaces

From the Street to Fashion Spaces

FROM SUBCULTURE TO HIGH FASHION

Streetwear was first introduced into high fashion in the 1980s by such designers as Katherine Hamnett and Jean Paul Gaultier, but the style has only broken through in the global fashion market over the last decade, becoming a norm in the industry.[7] One possible reason for this belated development might be that the zeitgeist has finally changed, and fashion is beginning to reflect new understandings in society. In the 1960s, the zeitgeist encompassed a heightened individualism, whereby people dressed in an 'alternative' manner and were less concerned about looking 'appropriate'.[8] In recent times, it can be argued that we have seen a similar development. The prevailing work culture has changed from one that prioritises a formalised and structured environment, with strict parameters around dress, to favouring a more creative and flexible workplace that calls for a less formal wardrobe. In particular, a recent tendency in many industries to see work and leisure as intertwined has caused overall dress codes in society to become more relaxed, making streetwear an increasingly popular option.[9] Many people now want to wear multi-purpose clothes that offer both comfort and durability, and streetwear fulfils this role perfectly.[10]

UNDERSTANDING THE HERITAGE OF STREETWEAR

Streetwear was created by skater culture and developed by hip-hop culture. This heritage might seem a long way from the catwalks, where the style is now so ubiquitous, and also from the backgrounds of the fashion critics who are now judging collections that employ street style's characteristics. Kanye West may well have had this disconnect in mind in 2017 when he moved the presentation of Yeezy Season 6 from the catwalks of New York Fashion Week to the streets of Calabasas, Los Angeles, as we learned in the case study 'Keeping Up with Changes'. By this act, West altered the significance of where and when a fashion show is presented, but equally importantly he also succeeded in bringing street style away from the catwalk and back to the streets.[11]

STREETWEAR AND SCANDINAVIA

Building on these lessons from Yeezy Season 6, we wanted to explore if it would be possible to launch a collection by an existing streetwear brand, such as Supreme, in a new location, Oslo, by developing a fashion show in an unusual location – a skatepark. The greatest challenge in this project is that Norway in general is not strongly associated with fashion. However, we would argue that its capital now has strong potential to be developed as a fashion space. The fashion industry has recently taken a direction that chimes with Scandinavian living, with its focus on comfort, simplicity and quality.[12] For example, a Nordic influence is very visible in the branding of Danish fashion label Ganni, which launched its Spring/Summer 2020 collection at Copenhagen Fashion Week in a tennis court. This unusual location communicated the sportiness of the region's lifestyles and fashion.[13] We believe that if a brand like Supreme were to launch

7   Brannon and Divita 2015, 82.
8   Brannon and Divita 2015, 223.
9   Ida Glosimot, 'Hvordan ble treningstøy high fashion?', Melk og Honning, 1 May 2017, https://melkoghonning.no/hvordan-ble-joggebuksa-trendy/; Elinor Block, 'The History of Streetwear: From Stussy to Vetements', Who What Wear, 27 October 2017, https://www.whowhatwear.co.uk/streetwear.
10 Glosimot 2017.
11 Steff Yotka, 'Can Yeezy's See-Me-Now-Buy-Now Paparazzi Proposition Work for Other Fashion Brands?', Vogue, 11 December 2017, https://www.vogue.com/article/yeezy-season-6-papparazzi-release.
12 Kate Finnigan, 'Nordic Chic: Eight Scandi Brands You Need to Know', The Telegraph, 30 January 2016, https://www.telegraph.co.uk/fashion/brands/nordic-chic-8-scandi-brands-you-need-to-know/.
13 Camilla Christensen, 'Ganni feiret ti år i København', Melk og Honning, 9 August 2019, https://melkoghonning.no/ganni-feiret-ti-ar-i-kobenhavn/.

Fashion Spaces

From the Street to Fashion Spaces

in Oslo, it would need to find a way to reflect how enthusiastically athleisure and street style have already been embraced in Scandinavia.

SKATEPARKS AS SITES FOR FASHION SPACES

When looking to develop a fashion space for a streatwear brand in Oslo, we chose to repurpose a skatepark in Majorstuen. As a site for a fashion show, this would reconnect streetwear to the street and communicate the brand's heritage, while also reflecting the importance of active lifestyles and the outdoors in Scandinavian fashion.[14] For the event, platforms would be added on both sides of the skatepark, changing the typology of the space. However, it would not be this expansion that turned the skatepark into a fashion space – only the fashion show itself would do that.

CONCLUSION

The visual stimuli provided by a skatepark would work well on social media – an important consideration for any fashion show. As it is a public place, we could rely on the interest of local residents to disseminate photographs and short videos of the show, allowing others to relive or reimagine the event through the metaspace created by these posts. The authenticity of the place, together with the local relevance of its outdoor location, should contribute to the narrative of the fashion space and reinforce the metaspace. As a result, the site helps to transfer important parts of the metaspace onto social media, making the fashion show last longer than just a handful of minutes in a skatepark.

14   Block 2017.

Sources

- Banham, Tom. 'The Story of Hip-Hop Style, from Run DMC to ASAP Rocky'. *Fashionbeans*, 6 October 2019. https://www.fashionbeans.com/article/hip-hop-style/#.
- Block, Elinor. 'The History of Streetwear: From Stussy to Vetements'. *Who What Wear*, 27 October 2017. https://www.whowhatwear.co.uk/streetwear.
- Brannon, Evelyn L. and Lorynn Divita. *Fashion Forecasting*, 4th ed. New York: Fairchild Books, 2015.
- Christensen, Camilla. 'Ganni feiret ti år i København'. *Melk og Honning*, 9 August 2019. https://melkoghonning.no/ganni-feiret-ti-ar-i-kobenhavn/.
- DeLeon, Jian. 'How Hip-Hop Left a Lasting Influence on Streetwear and Fashion'. *Highsnobiety*, 2 October 2018. https://www.highsnobiety.com/p/hip-hop-streetwear-fashion-influence/.
- Finnigan, Kate. 'Nordic Chic: Eight Scandi Brands You Need to Know'. *The Telegraph*, 30 January 2016. https://www.telegraph.co.uk/fashion/brands/nordic-chic-8-scandi-brands-you-need-to-know/.
- Glosimot, Ida. 'Hvordan ble treningstøy high fashion?'. *Melk og Honning*, 1 May 2017. https://melkoghonning.no/hvordan-ble-joggebuksa-trendy/.
- Icoolkid. 'The History of Streetstyle'. *Icoolkid.com*, 6 October 2019. https://www.icoolkid.com/article/history-streetwear.
- Lee, Jo Kwok Yee. 'Would Streetwear Really Be as Popular Without Hip Hop?'. *Streetwear Jobs*, 20 September 2018. https://streetwearjobs.com/history-of-streetwear-hiphop/.
- Yotka, Steff. 'Can Yeezy's See-Me-Now-Buy-Now Paparazzi Proposition Work for Other Fashion Brands?'. *Vogue*, 11 December 2017. https://www.vogue.com/article/yeezy-season-6-papparazzi-release.

From the Street to Fashion Spaces

Moving Beyond Gendered Spaces

Text
Daniel Jørgensen &
Martin Marthinius Tyri

Visuals
Daniel Jørgensen

GENDER-NEUTRAL FASHION

In fashion, the gender-neutral revolution is not a recent occurrence. Coco Chanel helped give women the freedom to wear trousers in the 1920s, and, from the peacock revolution of the 1960s onwards, musicians such as David Bowie, Prince and Kurt Cobain have blurred the line between the sexes.[1] These individuals may have been ahead of their time, but there has been an increasing acceptance of androgynous fashions over the last two decades. High fashion has embraced this movement with open arms, with luxury designers such as Rick Owens, Raf Simons and Gucci's Alessandro Michele eroding boundaries between the feminine and the masculine, thereby changing conversations around gender.[2] In 2016, Nicolas Ghesquière featured Jaden Smith wearing a skirt in a Louis Vuitton campaign, making Smith a global influencer for the gender-neutral movement.[3] Today, we are seeing more mainstream retailers – including H&M, Zara and Selfridges – following the example set by fashion houses and offering unisex collections.[4]

These developments mirror those in wider society. The social-media giant Facebook now has well over two billion active users, and these users can choose from around 60 gender options. Television shows are increasingly featuring regular or recurring LGBTQ+ characters, and there are growing numbers of celebrities who are open about their flexible

1 Maris Cohen, 'How Retail Is Becoming Less Gendered, and Why You Should Care', The NPD Group, 2015, https://www.npd.com/wps/portal/npd/us/news/tips-trends-takeaways/gender-neutral-retail/.
2 Sam Reed, 'How the Unisex Fashion Revolution Will Change the Way We Shop', *Hollywood Reporter*, 14 August 2017, https://www.hollywoodreporter.com/news/how-unisex-fashion-revolution-will-change-way-we-shop-1026995.
3 Erin Cunningham, 'Jaden Smith Lands an Unlikely Fashion Gig', *Refinery29*, 4 January 2016, https://www.refinery29.com/en-us/2016/01/100469/jaden-smith-louis-vuitton-campaign.
4 Priya Rao, 'Why Genderless Fashion Is So Important – and Why You Should Be Paying Attention', *Refinery29*, 4 August 2017, https://www.refinery29.com/en-us/2017/08/166515/genderless-unisex-fashion-trend.

Fashion Spaces

Moving Beyond Gendered Spaces

approach to gender. Larger companies are getting in on the act – a recent commercial for the Budweiser brand Bud Light declared that beer is for 'people of all genders'. In 2017, the state of California added a third gender option, 'non-binary', to identification documents such as drivers' licences and birth certificates, having already passed a bill requiring single-occupancy bathrooms to be gender-neutral the previous year. This erosion of binaries may, over time, result in significant changes in many areas of society, from relationships and sports to legal systems and the military.[5]

THE TRADITIONAL BRICKS-AND-MORTAR APPROACH

Although we're starting to get used to the concept of gender-neutral fashion, the vast majority of the industry's retail outlets have always divided their floor space by gender, and continue to do so today.[6] A man entering Zara will find the men's section and its associated fitting rooms together on the same floor, even if the latter are no longer labelled as men's – the signage will now merely say 'fitting rooms'. If a woman wants to try on men's clothing in these facilities, however, there's a strong chance that she will still be asked to use those in the women's section. Despite minor adjustments, the norms of gendered fitting rooms remain largely intact. For individuals identifying as transgender or non-binary, trying on clothes can be a judgemental and anxiety-ridden experience, making you constantly feel like you don't belong, and causing you to question your identity.[7]

EXPERIMENTS WITH GENDER-NEUTRAL RETAIL SPACES

A few retailers are now experimenting with gender-neutral retail spaces, some more successfully than others. We're going to look in detail at two that have taken a new approach. The first of these is Agender, a name chosen to signify 'without gender'. This 'shop within a shop' was located inside the London department store Selfridges, and made headlines when it opened in 2015. Agender was intended to reflect the emerging zeitgeist and reveal the future of genderless shopping. Its section of the store was marked out by mesh walls, an innovative design by Faye Toogood that ensured that Agender immediately attracted attention for the quality of its retail design, as well as for its progressive concept. Unfortunately, Agender shared its fitting rooms with other departments in Selfridges, thus it retained the traditional division between male and female facilities.[8] As a result, it ended up as little more than an outlet selling unisex clothing, undermining the promise of a genderless shopping experience, and failing to create a metaspace in which to imagine and reimagine gender-neutral fashion spaces.

The second example is The Phluid Project, a gender-neutral store in NoHo, New York, founded by Rob Smith. Having been sent away from a female clothing store when trying on clothes, Smith decided to create a modern, socially enlightened retail space that would provide an equal shopping experience for all genders. On launching in 2018, The Phluid Project was welcomed as the first of its kind, not just for the products it sold, but also for its success in creating a fusion of a genderless retail space, a community centre, and a platform for transgender and non-binary people. The store is divided by aesthetic instead

5 Katy Steinmetz, 'Behind the Time Cover Story: Beyond "He" or "She"', *Time*, 16 March 2017, https://time.com/4703058/time-cover-story-beyond-he-or-she/.

6 Katherine Bernard, 'Breaking the Binary', *New York Times*, 7 November 2018, https://www.nytimes.com/2018/07/11/style/phluid-project-nonbinary-fashion.html.

7 Lydia Smith, 'How the Rise of Genderless Shopping Is Transforming the Fashion Industry', *PinkNews*, 28 July 2018, https://www.pinknews.co.uk/2018/07/28/genderless-shopping-genderfluid-fashion/.

8 'Agender: The Concept Space', Selfridges & Co., accessed 8 November 2019, https://www.selfridges.com/SA/en/features/articles/content/agender-the-conceptspace/.

of gender, with open-to-all fitting rooms and gender-neutral mannequins – another first. With its combination of a diverse staff drawn from the local community, events on identity and activism, and a dedicated meeting space for community-based organisations, The Phluid Project has proved an ideal launch pad for the gender-neutral retail revolution.[9]

FLUID, OSLO

With our own proposal, Fluid, we wanted to design a solution that could transform a traditional department store into a more gender-neutral fashion space that would provide a gender-neutral shopping experience. For our case study, we chose a department store on Oslo's main street, Karl Johans gate, that currently maintains a very clear division between genders: the fashion departments are located on entirely separate floors alongside their respective fitting rooms, with womenswear on the first and second floors; menswear on the third floor; and the children's department on the fourth floor. So how could we make this traditional department store a less divided and more inclusive retail space? We explored different possibilities that might address the various challenges that transgender and non-gender people face while shopping. What would happen if we removed all gender division from the store? Or if we located all the store's fitting rooms on one shared floor? In the end our solution was to alter the entire first floor and turn it into a fluid shopping area for everyone. This would be achieved by combining a selection of menswear, womenswear and unisex clothing on this floor. In addition, the fitting rooms throughout

9   Mikelle Street, 'The World's First Gender-Neutral Store Just Opened in Manhattan', *I-D*, 22 March 2018, https://i-d.vice.com/en_us/article/7xdvxy/phluid-project-gender-neutral-store-new-york.

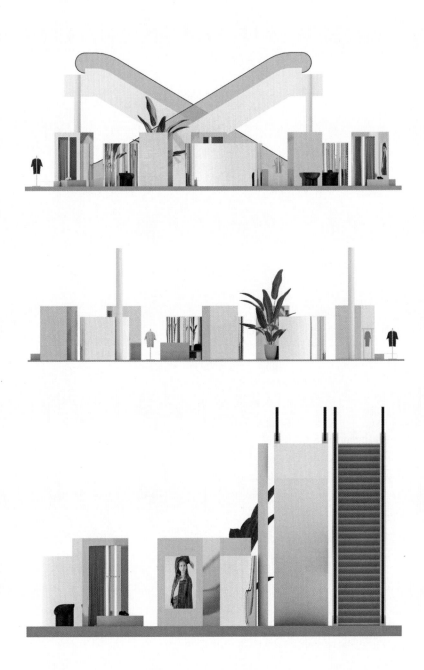

Moving Beyond Gendered Spaces

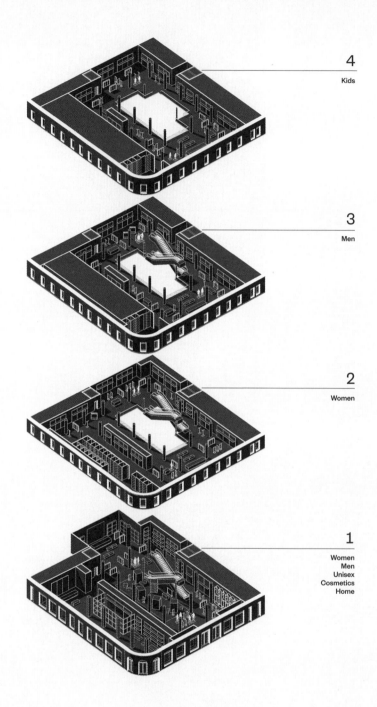

4
Kids

3
Men

2
Women

1
Women
Men
Unisex
Cosmetics
Home

Fashion Spaces

the store would be moved to the middle of each floor to act as focal points, and all of them would be turned into all-gendered spaces. The store could then offer gender-neutral shopping as an additional option, instead of removing areas dedicated to gendered clothing completely.

GENDER-NEUTRAL METASPACE

Using the conceptual model of fashion spaces proposed in this book, with its focus on location, place, site and metaspace, is it possible to develop a new metaspace that provides a gender-neutral fashion space? Although the model has mainly been discussed in relation to fashion shows, we feel that it could also be applied to retail spaces. In the case of our proposal, Fluid, its location is Oslo; its place is a gender-neutral retail outlet; and its site is the department store's architectural form. The moment that you enter this retail space and experience its gender-neutral shopping, you enter its metaspace, whether you are browsing the clothing or using the all-gender fitting rooms. By encouraging customers to share their gender-neutral experience on Instagram and other social-media platforms, the metaspace is expanded and prolonged, and a new dimension is added to the physical retail space.

CONCLUSION

As the gender-neutral movement becomes more mainstream, and younger consumers find gender and sexuality less relevant in their daily lives, it is clear that traditional retail spaces need to change. Bricks-and-mortar retail, which is already experiencing significant difficulties, needs to keep up with changes in both fashion and wider society, and open its doors to welcome new generations of shoppers. Achieving this transformation will require a different solution in every store, and each outlet must find its own approach that relates to both its layout and its concept. One thing we know for sure is that, one way or another, these changes have to be made. Every shop has the same power over whether it allows us to enter its metaspace or not. Hopefully, all of us will be able to enter every one of these metaspaces in the near future, and trying on clothes in stores will give us the freedom to develop our identities, regardless of gender and sexuality. It may well be that gendered clothing will become something of the past, just as traditional understandings of location, place and site are now beginning to lose their importance for fashion. The metaspace will be the starting point for us to decide not only our gender, but the location, place and site that we want to inhabit.

Sources

- Bernard, Katherine. 'Breaking the Binary'. *New York Times*, 7 November 2018. https://www.nytimes.com/2018/07/11/style/phluid-project-nonbinary-fashion.html.
- Cohen, Maris. 'How Retail Is Becoming Less Gendered, and Why You Should Care'. The NPD Group, 2015. https://www.npd.com/wps/portal/npd/us/news/tips-trends-takeaways/gender-neutral-retail/.
- Cunningham, Erin. 'Jaden Smith Lands an Unlikely Fashion Gig'. *Refinery29*, 4 January 2016. https://www.refinery29.com/en-us/2016/01/100469/jaden-smith-louis-vuitton-campaign.
- Rao, Priya. 'Why Genderless Fashion Is So Important – and Why You Should Be Paying Attention'. *Refinery29*, 4 August 2017. https://www.refinery29.com/en-us/2017/08/166515/genderless-unisex-fashion-trend.
- Reed, Sam. 'How the Unisex Fashion Revolution Will Change the Way We Shop'. *Hollywood Reporter*, 14 August 2017. https://www.hollywoodreporter.com/news/how-unisex-fashion-revolution-will-change-way-we-shop-1026995.
- Selfridges & Co. 'Agender: The Concept Space'. Selfridges & Co., accessed 8 November 2019. https://www.selfridges.com/SA/en/features/articles/content/agender-the-conceptspace/.
- Smith, Lydia. 'How the Rise of Genderless Shopping Is Transforming the Fashion Industry'. *PinkNews*, 28 July 2018. https://www.pinknews.co.uk/2018/07/28/genderless-shopping-genderfluid-fashion/.
- Steinmetz, Katy. 'Behind the Time Cover Story: Beyond "He" or "She"'. *Time*, 16 March 2017. https://time.com/4703058/time-cover-story-beyond-he-or-she/.
- Street, Mikelle. 'The World's First Gender-Neutral Store Just Opened in Manhattan'. *I-D*, 22 March 2018. https://i-d.vice.com/en_us/article/7xdvxy/phluid-project-gender-neutral-store-new-york.

Afterword: Archiving the Metaspace

Text
Vésma Kontere McQuillan

While researching the subject of fashion spaces, I found the proposition that fashion products can retain the memory of a metaspace an interesting one. Building on this possibility allows us to study fashion and architecture in a way that might help us understand metaspace as an intersection between the two disciplines, and as a result promote the generation of future fashion objects.

If we agree with the graphic designer Michael Rock that a fashion object is an ideal medium for design experimentation because of the limitations enforced by our anatomies, then the fashion show is an ideal medium for architectural experimentation because of its own spatial limitations. Rock stated that 'the design of a shoe is as much about *signification* as it is *function*, as much about *what it says* as *what it does*.'[1] The design of a fashion show is also about the meaning it conveys, because the fashion show is itself a reflection of wider culture.[2] And, since the space of the fashion show is controlled by architecture, we could state that, through an understanding of its metaspace, we might be able to touch the very essence of contemporary architecture and fashion: newness.

Vintage fashion objects can often be discussed in terms of fashioning memory. When collecting vintage pieces, we are consuming both the object and the image.[3] Similarly, at a contemporary fashion show, we consume both the object and the metaspace. Every Prada collection offers key pieces that will eventually become collectable, preserving that metaspace – Prada calls them 'archival objects'.[4] Pursuing these ideas, I sought out fashion objects from Prada's shows that both

1   Michael Rock and Stephanie Murg, *Pradasphere* (Milan: Progetto Prada Arte, 2014), 17.
2   Alexander Reichert, interview by Vésma Kontere McQuillan, Basel, 7 February 2017.
3   Heike Jenss, *Fashioning Memory: Vintage Style and Youth Culture*, Dress and Fashion Research (London: Bloomsbury Academic, 2015), 121.
4   Rock and Murg 2014, 13.

reimagine the metaspace and encapsulate the collection from which they come. These shows all happened in the same *location* (via Fogazzaro 36, Milan) and the same *place* (Prada's head-quarters) from 2000 until January 2018 (when they moved to the Fondazione Prada building at via Lorenzini 14), while their sites have been designed by the same architects (OMA/AMO) since 2004. Therefore, Prada's shows provide a rich archive for a comparative study of fashion spaces. As the only aspects susceptible to change are the site and the metaspace, it is possible to discover changes in society, culture and politics through the lens of Prada's evolving collections.

These insights will inform my forthcoming investigation into the ongoing collaboration between these two creative giants, *When Architecture Found Fashion: Prada + OMA/AMO*.

Sources

- Jenss, Heike. *Fashioning Memory: Vintage Style and Youth Culture*. Dress and Fashion Research. London: Bloomsbury Academic, 2015.
- Reichert, Alexander. Interview by Vésma Kontere McQuillan, Basel. 7 February 2017.
- Rock, Michael, and Stephanie Murg. *Pradasphere*. Milan: Progetto Prada Arte, 2014.

Fashion Spaces

Addendum: Further Research

Text
Vésma Kontere McQuillan

The essays and case studies featured in this book were researched and written in the two years before the COVID-19 pandemic began. In the following months, as we wrapped the book for publication, the global impact of the pandemic became clear, as did its implications for all industries and all areas of our lives, not least for the fashion industry and for architectural thinking around it. Much of the fashion industry is now moving online, and the development of virtual spaces is accelerating, requiring innovative social-media strategies and a strong focus on consumer interaction. At the same time, the pandemic is also reminding us of the importance of human contact in physical spaces. However, its future course remains uncertain, and its ultimate consequences are yet to be understood. Therefore, our team at Kristiania University College, Oslo, has now moved online and established the webzine nofilter.space as a site for further research. We look forward to seeing how fashion spaces will develop as we start to feel our way towards a new normal.

Editor & Contributors

Portraits
Iiro Piipponen, Tabea Treichel
& Kjeld Hansen

Vésma Kontere McQuillan

(b. 1970) is a Latvian-born architect and writer currently living in Norway, and is known for her architectural criticism for the Latvian daily press. For ten years from 1999, she worked as a journalist, columnist and blogger at the major Latvian-language daily newspaper *Diena*.

After relocating to Norway, she developed the concept and interior architecture for Oslo's first high-end department store, Eger Karl Johan, which opened in 2009. Since 2011, Vésma has been a professor at Kristiania University College, Oslo, where she developed the new retail design bachelor's degree. Students from this program are among the contributors to this publication.

She is the head of the research group ArchCommLab. Her research over the last five years has focused on the collaboration between OMA/AMO and Prada, looking in particular at the fashion shows created by AMO and Prada, and the design process behind these joint productions. This book is a direct outcome of this research.

In 2019, Vésma was appointed as guest editor for the Latvian architectural magazine *Latvijas Architektūra*, and produced the special issue 'Postmodernism after Postmodernism', for which she was awarded the best writer in the Architectural History category by the magazine.

Since 2020, she has been the host of a talk show for architects, *Trentini Talk Show*, and also the editor-in-chief of the webzine nofilter.space.

Editor & Contributors

Kjeld Hansen

(b. 1974) is an assistant professor at the ArchCommLab and the Mobile Technologies Lab of Kristiania University College, Oslo. He holds a master of science in information technology from the IT University of Copenhagen, and a bachelor of arts in communication studies from Roskilde University. Kjeld is currently enrolled at the PhD School at Copenhagen Business School, where he is researching the interplay between social media, mobile computing and information management in relation to public health and cities. Since 2020, he has been editor-at-large at the webzine nofilter.space.

Maren Bjelland

(b. 1998) is studying retail design at Kristiania University College, Oslo. She has over four years of experience in the retail industry, and has worked as a visual merchandiser. In 2019, she was on the scenography team for the Norwegian award show *Gullrutens Fagpris*.

Fashion Spaces

Mareike de Boer

(b. 1992) is a German retail and media designer who studied at the Peter Behrens School of Arts in Düsseldorf, and spent one semester at Kristiania University College, Oslo, as part of an exchange program. Prior to this, she completed three years of vocational training as a media designer and worked for two years at a media agency focused on concepts for the fashion industry. Mareike is currently pursuing a master's degree in interior architecture at the Peter Behrens School of Arts.

Katharina Brinkmann

(b. 1995) is studying retail design at the Peter Behrens School of Arts in Düsseldorf, and spent one semester at Kristiania University College, Oslo, as part of an exchange program. Before her studies, she completed three years of vocational training as a visual merchandiser at the German clothing company Ernsting's Family. She also has experience as an interior designer at a planning agency in Düsseldorf.

Ingrid Herstad

(b. 1996) is studying retail design at Kristiania University College, Oslo, having previously studied creative market communication for a year at its Bergen campus. She has experience as an interior designer at IKEA, and as a copywriter for Kristiania University College's advertising agency.

Vilde Aurora Johannessen

(b. 1997) is working at Tannum Møbler, an established design store in Oslo. She graduated in retail design from Westerdals, Kristiania University College, Oslo, in 2019. That summer, she studied at University of California, Berkeley, and completed an internship for a startup in San Francisco.

Daniel Jørgensen

(b. 1993) is studying retail design at Kristiania University College, Oslo. During his studies, he is working as a sales consultant in a furniture store. Before arriving at Kristiania University College, he worked for five years as a sales advisor and store manager at a men's clothing store.

Maren Bardine Lindseth

(b. 1994) is pursuing a master's degree in human-computer interaction at Kristiania University College, Oslo, having graduated in retail design from Westerdals, Kristiania University College, in 2019. Her current focus is on the e-health industry.

Elise Aurora Kjæran Pedersen

(b. 1995) is pursuing a master's degree in interior design at Nuova Accademia di Belle Art, Milan. She graduated in retail design from Westerdals, Kristiania University College, Oslo, in 2019.

Iiro Piipponen

(b. 1990) is pursuing a bachelor's degree in media content design at Lahti Institute of Design, Finland, and spent one semester at Kristiania University College, Oslo, as part of an exchange program. He is also working as a freelancer in the field of visual communication.

Tina Therese Rustadstuen

(b. 1996) is studying retail design at Kristiania University College, Oslo. During her studies, she is working part-time at a property-development company as an assistant interior architect, while also working at two shops.

Dawt Tha Tawk

(b. 1993) is studying retail design at Kristiania University College, Oslo. Previously, she studied interior design at Norges Interiørskole, Gjøvik, and she also has several years' experience working in the retail business.

Martin Marthinius Tyri

(b. 1995) is working at the Oslo showroom of the Danish furniture brand Alton&Heim. He graduated in retail design from Westerdals, Kristiania University College, Oslo, in 2019, having previously studied interior and spatial design at Edinburgh Napier University.

Notes

Credits

Fashion Spaces
A Theoretical View

Publisher
Frame

Editor
Vésma Kontere McQuillan

Authors
Vésma Kontere McQuillan
Kjeld Hansen
Maren Bjelland
Mareike de Boer
Katharina Brinkmann
Ingrid Herstad
Vilde Aurora Johannessen
Daniel Jørgensen
Maren Bardine Lindseth
Elise Aurora Kjæran Pedersen
Iiro Piipponen
Tina Therese Rustadstuen
Dawt Tha Tawk
Martin Marthinius Tyri

Production
Ana Martins

Copy Editor
John Jervis

Graphic Design
Barbara Iwanicka

Prepress
Edward de Nijs

Cover Photography
Courtesy of Prada

Printing
IPP Printers

Trade Distribution USA and Canada
Consortium Book Sales & Distribution, LLC.
34 Thirteenth Avenue NE, Suite 101
Minneapolis, MN 55413-1007
T +1 612 746 2600
T +1 800 283 3572 (orders)
F +1 612 746 2606

Trade Distribution Benelux
Frame Publishers
Domselaerstraat 27H
1093 JM Amsterdam
the Netherlands
distribution@frameweb.com
frameweb.com

Trade Distribution Rest of World
Thames & Hudson Ltd
181A High Holborn
London WC1V 7QX
United Kingdom
T +44 20 7845 5000
F +44 20 7845 5050

ISBN: 978-94-92311-48-1

© 2020 Frame Publishers, Amsterdam, 2020

The Koninklijke Bibliotheek lists this publication in the Nederlandse Bibliografie: detailed bibliographic information is available on the internet at http://picarta.pica.nl

Printed on acid-free paper produced from chlorine-free pulp. TCF ∞

Printed in the Poland

987654321